Thinking Critically:
Legalizing Marijuana

John Allen

ReferencePoint
Press®

San Diego, CA

About the Author

John Allen is a freelance writer living in Oklahoma City.

For more information, contact:
ReferencePoint Press, Inc.
PO Box 27779
San Diego, CA 92198
www. ReferencePointPress.com

Picture Credits:
Maury Aaseng: 9; Steve Zmina: 16, 21, 30, 34, 41, 48, 57, 62

LIBRARY OF CONGRESS CATALOGING-IN-PUBLICATION DATA

Allen, John.
  Legalizing marijuana / by John Allen.
    pages cm. — (Thinking critically)
  Includes bibliographical references and index.
  ISBN-13: 978-1-60152-782-0 (hardback)
  ISBN-10: 1-60152-782-9 (hardback) *199 7152*
  1. Marijuana—United States--Juvenile literature. 2. Marijuana—Law and legislation—United States—Juvenile literature. 3. Marijuana abuse—United States—Juvenile literature. 4. Drug legalization—United States—Juvenile literature. I. Title.
  HV5822.M3A45 2015
  362.29'50973—dc23
                                   2014030116

Contents

Foreword   4

Overview: Legalizing Marijuana   6

**Chapter One: Should Marijuana Be
Prescribed for Medical Use?**
The Debate at a Glance   12
Marijuana Should Be Prescribed for Medical Use   13
Marijuana Should Not Be Prescribed for Medical Use   19

**Chapter Two: Will Legalizing Marijuana
Lead to Increased Addiction?**
The Debate at a Glance   25
Legalizing Marijuana Will Lead to Increased Addiction   26
Legalizing Marijuana Will Not Lead to Increased Addiction   32

Chapter Three: Does Using Marijuana Present Health Risks?
The Debate at a Glance   38
Marijuana Use Presents Significant Health Risks   39
Marijuana Use Does Not Present Significant Health Risks   46

Chapter Four: Does Legalizing Marijuana Benefit Society?
The Debate at a Glance   52
Legalizing Marijuana Benefits Society   53
Legalizing Marijuana Does Not Benefit Society   59

Source Notes   65
Marijuana Facts   69
Related Organizations and Websites   72
For Further Research   76
Index   78

Foreword

"Literacy is the most basic currency of the knowledge economy we're living in today." Barack Obama (at the time a senator from Illinois) spoke these words during a 2005 speech before the American Library Association. One question raised by this statement is: What does it mean to be a literate person in the twenty-first century?

E.D. Hirsch Jr., author of *Cultural Literacy: What Every American Needs to Know*, answers the question this way: "To be culturally literate is to possess the basic information needed to thrive in the modern world. The breadth of the information is great, extending over the major domains of human activity from sports to science."

But literacy in the twenty-first century goes beyond the accumulation of knowledge gained through study and experience and expanded over time. Now more than ever literacy requires the ability to sift through and evaluate vast amounts of information and, as the authors of the Common Core State Standards state, to "demonstrate the cogent reasoning and use of evidence that is essential to both private deliberation and responsible citizenship in a democratic republic."

The Thinking Critically series challenges students to become discerning readers, to think independently, and to engage and develop their skills as critical thinkers. Through a narrative-driven, pro/con format, the series introduces students to the complex issues that dominate public discourse—topics such as gun control and violence, social networking, and medical marijuana. All chapters revolve around a single, pointed question such as Can Stronger Gun Control Measures Prevent Mass Shootings?, or Does Social Networking Benefit Society?, or Should Medical Marijuana Be Legalized? This inquiry-based approach introduces student researchers to core issues and concerns on a given topic. Each chapter includes one part that argues the affirmative and one part that argues the negative—all written by a single author. With the single-author format the predominant arguments for and against an issue can be synthesized into clear, accessible discussions supported by details and evidence including relevant facts, direct quotes, current examples, and statistical illustrations. All volumes include focus questions to guide students as they read each pro/con discussion, a list of key facts, and an annotated list of related organizations and websites for conducting further research.

The authors of the Common Core State Standards have set out the particular qualities that a literate person in the twenty-first century must have. These include the ability to think independently, establish a base of knowledge across a wide range of subjects, engage in open-minded but discerning reading and listening, know how to use and evaluate evidence, and appreciate and understand diverse perspectives. The new Thinking Critically series supports these goals by providing a solid introduction to the study of pro/con issues.

Legalizing Marijuana

On the first morning of 2014 consumers in Denver, Colorado, braved snow and biting cold to line up outside a store called Medicine Man. They were waiting to make history as the first customers in the United States to buy marijuana legally for recreational use. Once inside they were confronted by an array of marijuana strains in glass containers, many with fanciful names such as Alien Dawg Hybrid and Maui Sativa. For those who preferred to ingest the drug rather than smoke it, there were cannabis-infused candies and baked goods. The first purchasers left the store to cheers from onlookers and waiting customers. Similar scenes played out at each of the twenty-four shops across the state that were licensed and geared up to begin legal pot sales. Denver's mayor praised shop owners and buyers for behaving responsibly under the new law. For many activists, the day represented a shift toward sanity in the nation's drug policies. "This is what we worked so hard for the last few years," said Sean Azzariti, an Iraq War veteran who was the first purchaser at the 3D Cannabis Center in Denver. "It's mind-blowing."[1]

Not everyone was so enthusiastic. Denver police sent out a tweet asking people if they knew the law and emphasized that pot users could still be arrested for public consumption, driving while impaired, or offering the drug to a person under age twenty-one. Denver International Airport warned passengers against trying to take legally purchased marijuana home in their baggage. Many doctors, medical researchers, and addiction counselors were wary about the dangers of wider availability, especially for young people. Politicians and law enforcement experts fretted about marijuana's role as a so-called gateway drug that could lead to more dangerous substances. Even some patients using the drug as a prescribed painkiller were concerned that sales for recreational use would decrease the preexisting inventory for medical marijuana.

Overall, opponents' reactions ranged from eye-rolling skepticism to pronouncements of doom for the republic. As the experiment proceeded, news reports noted troubling incidents related to use by children and individuals with mental illness. Five months after Colorado's first legal sales, criticism was mounting. "I think, by any measure, the experience of Colorado has not been a good one unless you're in the marijuana business," said Kevin A. Sabet, the executive director of Smart Approaches to Marijuana, which opposes legalization. "We've seen lives damaged. We've seen deaths directly attributed to marijuana legalization. We've seen marijuana slipping through Colorado's borders. We've seen marijuana getting into the hands of kids."[2] Many observers predicted that the controversy was far from over, and that each side would continue to marshal evidence supporting its point of view on legalizing marijuana.

What Is Marijuana?

One reason for the controversy over legalization is marijuana's status as the most frequently used illegal drug in the world. Many view it as a substance that is basically harmless when used in moderation. The word *marijuana* refers to the dried flowers, seeds, stems, and leaves of the cannabis plant, which originated in south and central Asia and grows wild in many parts of the world. The shredded cannabis mixture is usually green, gray, or brown in color. On the street the drug goes by various names—as many as two hundred slang terms—including grass, weed, ganja, dope, reefer, roach, and Mary Jane. A related, stronger form is called hashish or hash. During the nineteenth century newspapers and medical journals almost always referred to the drug as cannabis. Some say the name change to *marijuana*, which began in the first decades of the twentieth century, had a racial basis. According to this theory, American officials sought to connect the drug to Mexican immigrants and other minorities. Thus, they employed the Mexican word to emphasize its dangerous effects as a "loco weed" used by outsiders. While the name shift might have played to prejudice against Hispanics, the US government was not alone in its worries about the drug's effects. Mexico actually prohibited the drug in 1920, seventeen years before the US government's ban.

Marijuana contains more than four hundred compounds. The high induced by using marijuana comes mainly from a chemical called delta-9-tetrahydrocannabinol (THC). This chemical has psychoactive properties—that is, it alters the user's mind. The strength, or potency, of marijuana depends on the amount of THC it contains, which can vary considerably from batch to batch. THC levels in marijuana ordinarily average about 5 percent, though there is evidence that potency has increased over the years. By comparison, hashish contains up to 20 percent THC. Another chemical in marijuana, cannabidiol (CBD), has a calming, sedative effect. Studies indicate it can relieve symptoms of nausea, anxiety, and convulsions.

The physical effects of using marijuana vary from person to person and also depend on how the drug is taken. Almost all users experience an altered mood. Whereas some may feel euphoric and grow more animated, others may become relaxed and mellow—the state described as feeling high or stoned. By altering the release of transmitters in the spinal cord, the THC in pot can bring pain relief. Some users notice a change in perceptions or a distortion of reality. Users generally have an increased heart rate, reduced blood pressure, and impaired short-term memory and concentration. Physical coordination is reduced. Smoking marijuana causes the eyes to redden and the mouth to become dry. Marijuana use also stimulates the appetite, a reaction known as the munchies. The effects of smoking pot subside in a few hours, but the drug can be detected in a person's body for weeks. Employers who must maintain a drug-free workplace administer urine tests to screen employees. A urine test usually can detect marijuana in a person's system up to two weeks after use.

How Marijuana Is Produced and Consumed

As an illegal narcotic in most of the United States, marijuana plants have to be cultivated in secrecy. Often pot is grown privately in small outdoor plots or greenhouse facilities. Authorities estimate that about one-third of America's marijuana crop is grown indoors. Larger crops are often

States with Legalized Marijuana for Medical or Recreational Use

The map shows states that allow marijuana use for medical or recreational purposes. Twenty-one states and the District of Columbia currently have legal marijuana in some form. Information is current up to April 22, 2014, and includes legalization measures approved in the 2012 elections that have yet to take effect.

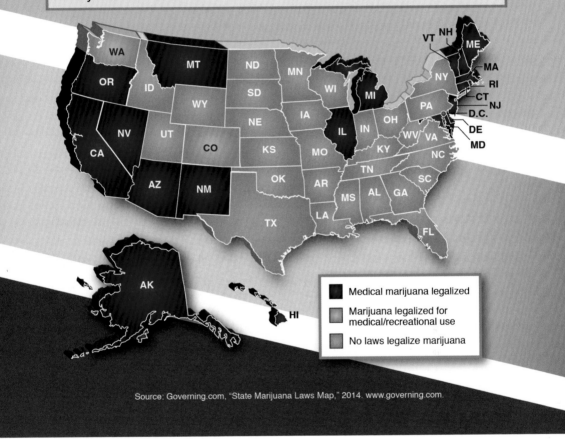

Source: Governing.com, "State Marijuana Laws Map," 2014. www.governing.com.

grown on remote farmlands or in forested areas. Once the plants are ready for harvest, the flowers are hung upside down to dry in a dark space at room temperature. The dried buds are then cured in glass jars and packaged. Some growers use ethanol to extract cannabinoids from leaves, stems, and buds, resulting in a product that can be mixed with food.

Marijuana is consumed in many different ways. According to the School of Public Health at the University of California, Berkeley, most users (including medical patients) "smoke the dried plant for the quickest effects; its active ingredients can also be delivered through capsules, vaporizers, mouth sprays, suppositories, liquid extracts, and foods and beverages."[3] Users typically smoke marijuana in hand-rolled cigarettes called joints or in water pipes called bongs or hookahs. In general, smoking small amounts of the drug is less harmful for casual users. Marijuana in other forms, such as baked goods and candies, may contain higher levels of THC and thus deliver more intense, and potentially more dangerous, effects.

The History of US Marijuana Laws

Authorities in the United States began to focus on marijuana's potential hazards during the first decades of the 1900s. Influenced by exaggerated antimarijuana propaganda such as the 1936 film *Reefer Madness*, the US Congress passed the Marihuana Tax Act in 1937, which regulated trafficking of the drug with heavy taxes. Harry J. Anslinger, the head of the US Treasury's Narcotics Bureau, wrote at the time, "How many murders, suicides, robberies, criminal assaults, holdups, burglaries and deeds of maniacal insanity it causes each year can only be conjectured."[4]

Attitudes began to change in the 1960s when the youth culture embraced drug use as a form of rebellion and a way to expand consciousness. Smoking pot became an accepted part of the hippie lifestyle. Debate raged about the harshness of laws against possession and whether the drug should be legalized. Congress responded with the Controlled Substances Act in 1970, which classified marijuana as a Schedule I drug, thus grouping it with the most dangerous narcotics and subjecting it to the most severe penalties. Nevertheless, several states reduced their penalties for marijuana possession, beginning with Oregon in 1973. In 1978 New Mexico passed the first state law recognizing marijuana's medical value. In the 1980s the Reagan administration instituted a so-called war on drugs that included laws requiring mandatory sentences for drug offenders. But again the pendulum swung back toward lenience in 1996

10

with the passage of California's Proposition 215. This law was the first major step toward legalization, allowing individuals to cultivate and use marijuana for medical purposes. By the middle of 2014 twenty-three states and the District of Columbia had passed laws legalizing medical marijuana, and two states—Colorado and Washington—allowed recreational use. Despite the trend toward legalization, the controversy shows no sign of abating. It includes important ideas about freedom, responsibility, and the character of American society in the future.

Chapter One

Should Marijuana Be Prescribed for Medical Use?

Marijuana Should Be Prescribed for Medical Use

- Marijuana has proven pain-relief benefits for patients suffering from painful illness.
- Medical marijuana is a good replacement for more problematic painkillers approved by the US Food and Drug Administration (FDA).
- Marijuana can decrease symptoms of nausea and vomiting in cancer patients undergoing chemotherapy.
- Marijuana's boost to the user's appetite can benefit patients who are losing too much weight.
- Marijuana can relieve muscle tremors and spastic movements associated with multiple sclerosis and paralysis.

The Debate at a Glance

Marijuana Should Not Be Prescribed for Medical Use

- Marijuana plants do not have measurable ingredients that are consistent from one dosage to the next.
- Marijuana use has side effects that are harmful to patients.
- There are other FDA-approved drugs for pain relief—some based on THC— that researchers consider safer and more reliable than marijuana.
- Marijuana has been overhyped as an effective treatment for a variety of conditions.
- Legalizing medical marijuana is just a step toward full legalization for recreational use.

Marijuana Should Be Prescribed for Medical Use

"I grew up like most of my generation believing that marijuana was something Satan was throwing at Americans, a communist plot. But I think most of us have come around to believe that marijuana is hugely beneficial when used correctly for medicinal purposes."

—Mehmet Oz is a surgeon, author, and teaching professor at Columbia University.

Quoted in Matt Ferner, "Dr. Oz Backs Medical Marijuana, Says It's 'Hugely Beneficial,'" *Huffington Post*, May 14, 2014. www.huffingtonpost.com.

Consider these questions as you read:

1. When you consider the facts and assertions in this discussion, how persuasive is the case that marijuana should be prescribed for medical use? Which facts and examples did you find most persuasive?
2. How has the FDA's labeling of marijuana as a Schedule I drug affected its acceptance for medical use? Explain your answer.
3. Should patients have the right to use a substance for medication even if some experts consider it to be potentially dangerous?

Editor's note: The discussion that follows presents common arguments made in support of this perspective, reinforced by facts, quotes, and examples taken from various sources.

Many physicians and researchers agree that medical marijuana is effective for pain management. It has been used to treat a variety of conditions, including AIDS, cancer, arthritis, migraines, glaucoma, back pain, and inflammation. It has even shown promise in treating the most challenging forms of chronic pain, such as neuropathic pain or nerve injuries. Endorsements for using medical marijuana to treat severe chronic pain have come from some of the most prestigious health organizations, such as the American Academy of Family Physicians, the American Public Health Association, the American Nurses Association, and the *New England Journal of Medicine*. Experts emphasize that patients deserve the opportunity to make their own choices about pain relief. In a groundbreaking 1997 editorial, Dr. Jerome P. Kassirer wrote in the *New England Journal of Medicine*, "I believe that a federal policy that prohibits physicians from alleviating suffering by prescribing marijuana for seriously ill patients is misguided, heavy-handed, and inhumane."[5] Kassirer also called for marijuana to be recategorized from a dangerous narcotic to a drug with proven medical utility.

Much of the medicinal value in marijuana comes from THC, one of the chemicals called cannabinoids. These cannabinoids link to a person's own natural system of endocannabinoids, which regulate the body's responses to pain, hunger, and other stimuli. Thus, THC reinforces receptors in the body and brain and produces healthful effects such as a reduction in the experience of pain. These benefits agree with descriptions of medical marijuana in different cultures going back five thousand years. In the 1800s marijuana—under its scientific name, cannabis—was commonly prescribed in the United States for pain relief and sedation. Today, although much research remains to be done—mainly because of marijuana's unwarranted federal status as a Schedule I "dangerous" narcotic—more and more studies are showing the drug's potential for pain relief. Typical is the recent study of two hundred patients at the University of Colorado's Spine Center. "According to the users, marijuana worked," writes medical reporter John Fauber. "A total of 89% said it greatly or moderately relieved their pain, and 81% said it worked as well or better than narcotic painkillers."[6]

As more states legalize the drug for clinical use, the evidence in favor of medical marijuana continues to grow. A Fox News poll released in May 2013 showed that 85 percent of US voters favor the use of marijuana for medical purposes. The renowned neurosurgeon and health advocate Sanjay Gupta recently announced he had changed his opinion about medical marijuana. "It doesn't have a high potential for abuse, and there are very legitimate medical applications. In fact, sometimes marijuana is the only thing that works."[7] Ben Pollara, a political consultant who manages Florida's United for Care initiative, sees no downside to medical marijuana as a pain reliever. "If you look at the public opinion data, of which there is quite a bit, it is socially and politically acceptable as it is . . . it's kind of a no brainer," says Pollara. "Grandma's sick? Pot can help her? Why not? If you know somebody who's in pain and there's a glimmer of hope that medical marijuana can relieve their suffering, it's a pretty stone cold person that doesn't think it should be allowed."[8]

Better than Narcotic Painkillers

Medical marijuana is safer and less addictive than many substances that are prescribed for pain relief in large numbers today and often abused, including opiates such as morphine and codeine. At the very least, adding medical marijuana to a regimen of these prescription painkillers can lead to lower doses of the opiates and fewer side effects. Patients can thus reduce chronic pain while also reducing the risk of overdose and addiction. As author Mark Collen notes in a 2012 peer-reviewed study in the *Harm Reduction Journal*, about sixty-five thousand people died from opiate painkiller overdose between 1999 and 2006, but no one has ever died

> "If you know somebody who's in pain and there's a glimmer of hope that medical marijuana can relieve their suffering, it's a pretty stone cold person that doesn't think it should be allowed."[8]
>
> —Ben Pollara, a political consultant who manages Florida's United for Care initiative.

from an overdose of cannabis. Commentators also report that cannabis and opiates can interact to produce even more pain-relief benefits. Until recently most doctors were reluctant to prescribe cannabis and opiates together, even if medical marijuana was legal in their state. But studies show that vaporized cannabis administered with morphine and oxycodone can augment their painkilling effect. With regard to nerve pain, medical marijuana may be even more beneficial. Strong doses of opiates are required to achieve even slight nerve pain relief. Some doctors believe that medical marijuana may be an effective substitute for opiates in treating nerve pain; although much more research is needed, early studies have shown

Most Americans Say Marijuana Has Legitimate Medical Uses

Americans of all age groups and political beliefs now realize the proven benefits of medical marijuana. Even respondents who are sixty-five and older acknowledge its legitimate medical uses. As more states legalize pot for clinical use, support continues to grow.

Does marijuana have legitimate medical uses?*			
	Does %	Does not %	Don't know %
Total	**77**	**16**	**7**
18–29	84	12	4
30–49	81	14	5
50–64	77	17	6
65+	60	23	16
Republican	72	20	8
Democrat	76	16	8
Independent	82	13	5

Source: The Pew Research Center for the People & the Press, "Older Americans Say Marijuana Has Legitimate Medical Uses," April 4, 2013. www.people-press.org.

*Figures may not add up to 100% due to rounding.

promise for such treatments. Overall, medical marijuana could be a helpful supplement or an effective replacement for opiate-based prescription painkillers that have dangerous side effects.

Effective Against Nausea and Vomiting

Medical marijuana's ability to relieve symptoms of nausea and vomiting is well established, going back to research in the 1970s. This makes it an ideal medication for patients undergoing chemotherapy. Vomiting can lead to dehydration and weight loss in cancer patients. Severe side effects associated with chemotherapy and radiation therapy can make patients reluctant to even begin the treatments, so dealing with these side effects is crucial. Anne Johnston, age fifty-six, was diagnosed with stage III colorectal cancer and suffered severe side effects from chemotherapy, including nausea, vomiting, and fatigue. Johnston tried several antinausea drugs with no success. Then a friend suggested she try smoking pot for relief. "I had about three hits off of the joint," says Johnston. "All of a sudden—the pain was gone, the nausea was gone. . . . I was feeling like how a normal person should."[9] Medical marijuana also can reduce nausea from migraines and from the use of powerful opiate-related painkillers such as oxycodone. Research indicates that smoking the drug is more effective than ingesting it orally to get the best antinausea results.

A Boost to the Appetite

The cliché about how marijuana stimulates the appetite has important applications for cancer and AIDS patients. An improved appetite can help patients consume enough calories to avoid severe weight loss and loss of energy—the sense of wasting away. Studies show that medical marijuana heightens the patient's ability to taste and smell food, making eating more pleasurable than it would be otherwise. Marinol, a synthetic drug that contains THC, already has approval from the FDA for boosting appetite in HIV patients. Many patients prefer smoking pot to taking Marinol in pill form because of the increased ability to vary the dosage. Medical marijuana may also have value for treating those with anorexia nervosa and other eating disorders. Anorexia nervosa is a condition in which subjects have an intense fear of gaining weight and a distorted body image and thus refuse to maintain a healthy body weight. Medical marijuana could stimulate the appetites of such sufferers and relieve their stress at mealtimes.

> "I had about three hits off of the joint. All of a sudden—the pain was gone, the nausea was gone. . . . I was feeling like how a normal person should."[9]
>
> —Anne Johnston, a cancer patient undergoing chemotherapy.

Relief for Muscle Tremors and Spasms

Yet another application for medical marijuana is treatment for tremors and spasms associated with conditions such as multiple sclerosis (MS), Parkinson's disease, and paralysis. MS is a disease of the central nervous system that affects about 2.5 million people worldwide and affects women more than twice as often as men. The chronic pain, muscle stiffness, and muscle spasms that are common symptoms of MS may be treatable by some forms of cannabis. Marijuana's proven ability to relieve inflammation and provide a relaxing effect has drawn the interest of MS researchers in several states. Doctors in Massachusetts say that a study by the American Academy of Neurology shows promise for treating certain MS symptoms with marijuana. According to Dr. Howard Weiner, the director of the Partners MS Center at Harvard Medical School, "I think it is a positive finding, and it makes me feel more comfortable telling patients to use medical marijuana."[10] The National Multiple Sclerosis Society is on record in support of patients' rights to consult with health care providers to receive marijuana as a treatment provided it is legally available in their states. The group favors doing further research on medical marijuana to better understand its benefits and potential risks.

Tremors and muscle rigidness associated with Parkinson's disease may also respond to marijuana treatment. Trial data from a study by researchers at Tel Aviv University in Israel shows that smoking marijuana offered patients significant improvement in muscle trembling and rigidity and also allowed for better sleep. Such results lead some investigators to predict that medical marijuana may have value in treating other neurological diseases such as Tourette's syndrome and epilepsy.

Marijuana Should Not Be Prescribed for Medical Use

"What there's a huge demand for is marijuana. Not medical marijuana. Because when we run a medically based program, you don't see the demand. . . . This program and all these other programs, in my mind, are a front for legalization."

—Chris Christie, governor of New Jersey.

Quoted in Brent Johnson, "Christie Says Medical Marijuana Programs Are 'a Front for Legalization,'" *Star-Ledger*, June 17, 2014. www.nj.com.

Consider these questions as you read:

1. Do you agree that problems with consistent dosage for medical marijuana are a major argument against its use? Why or why not?
2. Judging from evidence here, are marijuana's side effects too severe for it to be used as a medication? Explain.
3. Do you think legalizing medical marijuana will lead inevitably to legalization of recreational marijuana? Explain.

Editor's note: The discussion that follows presents common arguments made in support of this perspective, reinforced by facts, quotes, and examples taken from various sources.

A key drawback to using the marijuana plant for medical purposes is the fact that it varies in potency and chemical makeup. This makes it virtually impossible to control dosage properly. (*Dosage* is the exact amount of a medicine to be taken at one time or at intervals over a period of time.) The hundreds of chemical compounds found in marijuana vary widely from plant to plant and can produce different—and unpredictable—effects on users. As the National Institute on Drug Abuse (NIDA) observes, "To be considered a legitimate medicine by the FDA, a substance must have well-defined and measurable ingredients that are consistent from one unit (such as a pill or injection) to the next."[11] Marijuana simply does not have that kind of consistency. Pharmaceutical companies spend millions of dollars to ensure that their drugs are manufactured with precise ingredients and dosages. If marijuana cannot meet these ordinary standards, it should not be prescribed for medical use.

The problems with consistent dosage are made worse by smoking the drug. In the world of medicine, the idea of smoking any substance tends to be looked at skeptically. Pharmaceutics professor Mahmoud ElSohly, who administers the University of Mississippi's Marijuana Project, declares, "There's an inherent problem with the smoking of marijuana as a delivery system." He adds, "There are so many variables in the smoking process. It's ludicrous to think you could come up with a dosage."[12] ElSohly points out that low levels of THC generally produce the most medicinal benefits, such as appetite stimulation and anxiety relief. Approved medications based on THC, such as Marinol, contain low doses of the chemical. Yet ElSohly's research indicates that the THC content in street pot, and in much pot sold as medical marijuana, is increasing in the United States. THC levels that averaged 1 or 2 percent during the 1970s are about 6 percent today and up to 12 percent in some high-potency varieties. High levels of THC would be difficult for even experienced smokers to tolerate, says ElSohly. Patients subjected to such dosages might experience the opposite of the desired effect, such as severe nausea and heightened anxiety. Doctors should not prescribe any medication for which the results are so unpredictable.

A Dangerous Drug with Harmful Side Effects

Marijuana remains a dangerous drug with no medical benefits and a high potential for abuse. That is according to federal law: the Controlled Substances Act of 1970. As a so-called Schedule I drug, marijuana is grouped with substances such as heroin, ecstasy, and LSD—not exactly the contents of a typical medicine cabinet. While some question whether pot belongs in this category, the fact remains that Schedule I drugs are consid-

Questionable Reasons for Medical Marijuana Use

Among people who use medical marijuana dispensaries nationwide, only a tiny percentage seeks the drug for HIV, cancer, or glaucoma—three conditions for which marijuana supposedly is an ideal treatment. Most obtain pot for the vague complaint of "chronic pain," a questionable use.

Why Do People Use Medical Marijuana?	
Disorder that requires treatment	Reason for medical marijuana use
Chronic pain	58.2%
Mental health disorders	22.9%
Sleep disorders	21.3%
Neurological disorders	16.6%
HIV	1.6%
Cancer	1.5%
Glaucoma	1.3%

Source: Pacific Southwest Addiction Technology Transfer Center, "Medical Marijuana: What HIV Providers Need to Know," 2013. http://paetc.org.

ered hazardous and are not to be prescribed or dispensed. Advocates for medical marijuana typically describe the drug as virtually harmless, but the truth is that pot has many harmful side effects. The large number of doctors who resist climbing on the medical marijuana bandwagon have valid concerns about these side effects, and they insist that the drug's drawbacks outweigh its supposed benefits to patients.

Smoking marijuana, whether for medicinal or recreational purposes, subjects the user to an increased risk of lung problems, including emphysema. Marijuana has four times the tar and 40 percent more cancer-causing agents than tobacco. Smoking pot can also worsen upper respiratory problems such as asthma. While medical marijuana is supposed to benefit those suffering from immune-system diseases such as HIV/AIDS, the truth may be the opposite. A 2010 study published in the *European Journal of Immunology* found that marijuana can trigger production of cells that actually suppress the body's immune system, making patients more vulnerable to cancer and infection. Research published in June 2014 by Boston's Beth Israel Deaconess Medical Center showed that in the first hour of smoking marijuana a user's heart attack risk was five times greater than that of a nonsmoker. A 2014 French study found a link between cardiovascular events (heart attacks and strokes) and regular marijuana users. In an editorial about the study in the *Journal of the American Heart Association*, Dr. Sherief Rezkalla and Dr. Robert A. Kloner cite evidence that marijuana use increases clotting agents in the blood and can impede blood flow in tiny vessels to the heart and brain. The doctors asked, "Do we really know enough about the cardiovascular effects of marijuana to feel comfortable about its use in patients with known cardiovascular disease or patients with cardiovascular risk factors?"[13] These newly found risks accompany the already well-known side effects of using marijuana, including insomnia, drowsiness, short-term memory loss, impaired perception and problem solving, and anxiety or uneasiness. When looked at with a clinical eye, medical marijuana has a significant downside that doctors find troubling.

> "Do we really know enough about the cardiovascular effects of marijuana to feel comfortable about its use in patients with known cardiovascular disease or patients with cardiovascular risk factors?"[13]
>
> —Dr. Sherief Rezkalla and Dr. Robert A. Kloner, in an editorial in the *Journal of the American Heart Association.*

Other Drugs Are Better than Smoking Marijuana

Smoking pot as medicine is unnecessary because there are other drugs available that are safer and more effective. Some of these drugs contain the cannabinoids THC and/or CBD. These are the chemicals in the marijuana plant that are touted for their medicinal benefit. For example,

Marinol contains THC and is an effective treatment for nausea due to chemotherapy and for extreme weight loss caused by AIDS. Sativex, a mouth spray that contains roughly equal parts THC and CBD, has been approved in Europe to treat spasms associated with MS and is in clinical trials for US approval. These drugs are manufactured with the precise dosages that give physicians confidence in prescribing them. "It is clear to anyone following this story that it is possible to develop marijuana-based medications in accordance with modern scientific standards, and many more such legitimate medications are just around the corner,"[14] says Kevin A. Sabet, chief of the University of Florida's Drug Policy Institute.

There are also more traditional pain-relief medicines, including over-the-counter drugs such as acetaminophen and ibuprofen and prescription medications such as codeine. Although patients respond differently to different drugs, the effectiveness of these traditional pain relievers is well documented. Similarly, to combat nausea there are prescription drugs as well as effective home remedies, such as the use of ginger, that do not carry marijuana's side effects.

Marijuana Is Overhyped as a Medicine

Supporters of medical marijuana make miraculous claims for its value as a medication, yet many of these claims do not bear up under scrutiny. For example, it has long been touted as a treatment for glaucoma, a disease that damages the optic nerve and can lead to blindness. Yet no less an authority than the Glaucoma Research Foundation (GRF) rejects this idea. According to Henry D. Jampel, a professor of ophthalmology writing on the GRF website, although smoking marijuana can indeed lower eye pressure associated with the disease, its effects last only three to four hours a day, meaning that a patient would have to smoke six to eight times a day for around-the-clock relief. In addition, marijuana also lowers blood pressure, which can reduce blood flow to the optic nerve and possibly cause damage. "The take-home message," writes Jampel, "is that although marijuana can lower the eye pressure, recommending this drug in any form for the treatment of glaucoma at the present time does not make sense given its side effects and short duration of action, coupled with a lack of evidence that its use alters the course of glaucoma."[15]

Similarly, a study by McGill University researchers in Montreal, Canada, concludes that marijuana is not an effective option for treating arthritis pain. The authors of the study found that marijuana does not work well with arthritis patients because the pain pathways are different from those in other diseases.

A Step Toward Full Legalization

Many advocates of medical marijuana simply want to speed the process of full legalization for recreational use. They believe that if pot is seen as a medicine with all sorts of beneficial effects, it will more readily be accepted as a fully legal substance. Also, research shows that many users of medical marijuana may not have serious medical conditions at all. A 2012 study indicates that only 10 percent of Californians with medical marijuana cards actually have cancer, AIDS, or MS—the conditions for which pot is supposedly the ideal treatment. Nevertheless, public acceptance of medical marijuana is widespread and growing. Marijuana advocates in Colorado pointed to the state's success with its regulated medical pot market in their campaign for legalization. The push to legalize medical marijuana has become a convenient stepping-stone to legalizing pot for casual use.

"Recommending this drug in any form for the treatment of glaucoma at the present time does not make sense given its side effects and short duration of action, coupled with a lack of evidence that its use alters the course of glaucoma."[15]

—Henry D. Jampel, a professor of ophthalmology at Johns Hopkins.

Chapter Two

Will Legalizing Marijuana Lead to Increased Addiction?

Legalizing Marijuana Will Lead to Increased Addiction

- Regular use of marijuana over long periods often leads to psychological dependence on the drug.
- Heavy users require more and more marijuana to achieve the same high.
- Research indicates that heavy marijuana use can produce withdrawal symptoms when a user tries to stop.
- Marijuana is a gateway drug that can lead to experimentation with other drugs that are addictive.

The Debate at a Glance

Legalizing Marijuana Will Not Lead to Increased Addiction

- Marijuana is not physically addictive and is psychologically addictive only for a small percentage of heavy users.
- Despite already being the most widely used illicit substance in the world, marijuana has been linked to dependence in less than 10 percent of users.
- Research indicates that marijuana is not a gateway drug that leads to the use of more addictive substances such as cocaine, heroin, or crystal meth.
- Legalizing marijuana actually may decrease addiction since users no longer will need to seek out illegal dealers peddling more dangerous drugs along with marijuana.

Legalizing Marijuana Will Lead to Increased Addiction

"You can become dependent upon cannabis; it meets all the criteria for substance use disorder. The people who show up for treatment for cannabis tend to have the same problems as those who have alcohol, tobacco, or cocaine problems, and their success quitting is no better: anywhere from 5 to 40 percent at the end of treatment."

—Dr. Ryan Vandrey, assistant professor of psychiatry at Johns Hopkins School of Medicine's Behavioral Pharmacology Research Unit.

Quoted in Mat Edelson, "Johns Hopkins Expert Shares His Thoughts on the Legalization of Marijuana," *Johns Hopkins Gazette*, March 6, 2014. http://hub.jhu.edu.

Consider these questions as you read:

1. From the evidence presented, do you agree that marijuana is physically or psychologically addictive? Why or why not?
2. How serious is the problem of heavy users requiring more and more marijuana to get the same effect? Explain.
3. How persuasive is the contention that marijuana is a so-called gateway drug? Explain.

Editor's note: The discussion that follows presents common arguments made in support of this perspective, reinforced by facts, quotes, and examples taken from various sources.

Despite what many people believe, marijuana is addictive. Estimates cited by NIDA suggest that about 9 percent of regular users become addicted to pot. Among users who begin young, the estimates rise to 17 percent, and among those who use pot daily, they are more than 25 percent and perhaps as high as 50 percent. The most recent data indicate that more than 4 million Americans meet the criteria for marijuana addiction. Since legalizing marijuana will undoubtedly lead to more new users and more frequent use, concerns about increased addiction are legitimate. In fact, the US National Library of Medicine says that marijuana dependence is already more common than other drug dependencies strictly because of the greater number of people who use pot. Adding to the number of regular users through legalization will only make the problem worse.

Many users fall into addiction almost imperceptibly after smoking marijuana for a long period. A young man named Paul tells a typical story to the Foundation for a Drug-Free World:

> I started using on a lark, a dare from a best friend who said that I was too chicken to smoke a joint and drink a quart of beer. I was fourteen at that time. After seven years of using and drinking I found myself at the end of the road with addiction. I was no longer using to feel euphoria, I was just using to feel some semblance of normality. Then I started having negative feelings about myself and my own abilities. . . . I became so paranoid that I successfully drove everyone away and found myself in the terrible place no one wants to be in—I was alone. I'd wake up in the morning and start using and keep using throughout the day.[16]

Because marijuana addiction involves more of a psychological dependence on the drug rather than the strong physical dependency associated with narcotics such as heroin, those who support legalization tend to minimize its effects. They view psychological cravings as more manageable. However, experts on addiction disagree. "The distinction is completely arbitrary," says Dr. Nora Volkow, the director of NIDA. "Psychological addiction occurs in your brain and it's a physical change."[17]

Requiring More Pot to Get the Same High

A key sign of marijuana abuse is the need to smoke more in order to get the same effect. Frequent use of marijuana, as with other substances that

27

produce a euphoric effect, can foster a tolerance to the drug, rendering the user less responsive to it. Over a long period high dosages of THC and other cannabinoids can clog, or desensitize, the cannabinoid receptors in the brain, thus reducing marijuana's pain-relieving and relaxing effects. This, in turn, results in a user smoking more and often searching for more potent weed. It becomes more difficult to achieve the desired state of relaxation or mild euphoria. Users suddenly find themselves smoking much more of the drug than intended, and they are unable to cut down on marijuana use. What began as a casual habit can spiral into a life-altering obsession with frequent episodes of anxiety and even paranoia. Those who have used the drug in increasing amounts for prolonged periods can also experience marijuana burnout—a sluggish condition in which they become dull, slow moving, and unresponsive to friends.

> "I became so paranoid that I successfully drove everyone away and found myself in the terrible place no one wants to be in—I was alone. I'd wake up in the morning and start using and keep using throughout the day."[16]
>
> —A young marijuana user named Paul, quoted by the Foundation for a Drug-Free World.

Significantly, even many marijuana advocates suggest that heavy users take occasional tolerance breaks of total abstinence to guard against becoming too desensitized to the drug. This shows the force of the drug's grip. "Essentially, the key to a successful tolerance break," writes blogger and longtime marijuana user Kristin Mastre, "is reminding yourself that cannabis is best used as a different way to experience life, not as the reason to experience life. The first day of a cannabis tolerance break feels interminable; everything makes you want to smoke. The second day feels a little better (if you manage to get to sleep the night before)."[18] Such breaks will be harder to accomplish for weak-willed users when there is a shop down the street offering several varieties of marijuana for sale. Thus, legalizing marijuana will result in more problems related to increased tolerance or desensitization. For many heavy users, this will lead to a harmful and obsessive quest for the perfect high.

Withdrawal Symptoms

It is well documented that marijuana users who try to stop using the drug experience serious withdrawal symptoms. According to NIDA, "Long-term marijuana users trying to quit report withdrawal symptoms including irritability, sleeplessness, decreased appetite, anxiety, and drug craving, all of which can make it difficult to abstain [from taking the drug]."[19] Research indicates that those who experience insomnia and mood swings tend to relapse into using again more often than those with other symptoms. Pot advocates stress that marijuana withdrawal is not nearly as strenuous as withdrawal from more dangerous substances such as heroin. Yet the symptoms of marijuana withdrawal are certainly harsh enough to cause many who are trying to quit to resume using it in order to relieve the symptoms. Research shows that daily smokers exhibit the most symptoms, but even those who smoke less than once a week experience moderate withdrawal symptoms that cannot be ignored.

The most frequently reported withdrawal symptom for users trying to quit is a craving for marijuana, with one study showing three-quarters of participants experiencing an intense desire for the drug. Craving is a common feature of other addictions, including heroin, opium, alcohol, and nicotine. Probably the second most common symptom for marijuana withdrawal is severe mood swings, from depression and irritability to euphoria and back. Mood swings can persist from a few weeks to several months. One of the most difficult symptoms to handle is sleep disruption. This can include insomnia, restlessness, and nightmares. Nearly half of those trying to quit experience sleep problems. Former users sometimes have dreams about smoking weed years after they have quit. Among other withdrawal symptoms are headaches, fatigue, digestion problems, night sweats, trembling, and dizziness.

David Allsop of the National Cannabis Prevention and Information Centre in New South Wales, Australia, completed an influential study about marijuana withdrawal in 2012. Allsop points out that withdrawal can affect everything from a former user's job performance to the ability to carry out daily routines. Allsop believes that the public is generally not well informed about pot addiction. "I suspect that there is a long way to

Marijuana Is Top Gateway Drug for Teens

Although marijuana is still illegal in most states, and remains illegal for teenagers in all states, it is the most frequently used gateway drug for teens. Among teens who try illicit, addictive drugs, more than half try marijuana first. Painkillers, the next most frequent choice, are a distant second. Once marijuana is legalized it will be more widely available and even easier for teens to obtain, increasing the likelihood of addiction problems among teens.

2.9 Million Initiates of Illicit Drugs

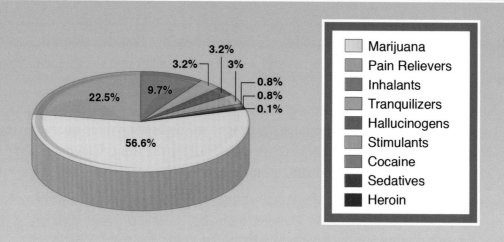

Source: Parentingteens.com. "Teen Substance Abuse Statistics, Charts and Graphs," March 18, 2013. www.parentingteens.com.

go still in changing the popular beliefs," Allsop says. Educating people that withdrawal from marijuana "makes you irritable, tense and anxious, and disrupts your sleep is one good place to gain some traction,"[20] he adds.

A Gateway Drug

Legalization advocates have strived to convince the public that marijuana use does not lead to harder drugs. Clinical studies, however, indicate that pot might indeed be a gateway drug to other substance abuse. For example, a 2012 study by researchers at the Yale University School of Medicine showed that marijuana use was linked to prescription drug abuse in men and women aged eighteen to twenty-five. The study found that subjects who had used marijuana were 2.5 times more likely than non-users to move on to prescription painkillers. But even more troubling is the risk for young people exposed to legal marijuana use in households. Substance abuse expert Mike Gimbel says, "Eighty percent of addiction is due to environment. So, especially for children, if they are exposed to an environment where people are drinking or smoking pot, they are much more likely to enter a world where they can find drugs like heroin or cocaine. So, I consider marijuana a social gateway drug."[21] The dangers to children and adolescents of having marijuana products in a household environment are already showing up in Colorado. In April 2014 Dr. Michael Distefano of Children's Hospital Colorado testified that seven juveniles had been treated there for acute illnesses due to consuming potent edible forms of pot. Doubtless problems with adolescent substance abuse and later addiction will only grow more serious as Colorado's experiment with legalization continues.

"Eighty percent of addiction is due to environment. So, especially for children, if they are exposed to an environment where people are drinking or smoking pot, they are much more likely to enter a world where they can find drugs like heroin or cocaine. So, I consider marijuana a social gateway drug."[21]

—Dr. Michael Distefano of Children's Hospital Colorado.

Legalizing Marijuana Will Not Lead to Increased Addiction

"Obviously, the vast majority of marijuana users are neither addicted nor almost addicted to cannabis. Their use doesn't escalate over time, they can enjoy its effects without endangering some major element of their lives."

—J. Wesley Boyd, an attending psychiatrist at Cambridge Health Alliance.

J. Wesley Boyd, "Is Marijuana Addictive?," *Psychology Today*, November 3, 2013. www.psychologytoday.com.

Consider these questions as you read:

1. Do you think marijuana should be considered addictive if it results in a psychological dependence but not a physical one? Explain.
2. Do you think dependency rates for marijuana users will remain about the same in places where it is legally available? Why or why not?
3. Advocates for marijuana legalization insist that smoking pot does not lead to using harder drugs any more than tobacco or alcohol does. Do you agree or disagree? Explain.

Editor's note: The discussion that follows presents common arguments made in support of this perspective, reinforced by facts, quotes, and examples taken from various sources.

Marijuana is not physically addictive; that is, it does not have any biological properties that lead to physical dependence. Withdrawal from the drug involves few of the physical symptoms associated with ceasing to use more potent substances such as heroin or cocaine. Even alcohol and nicotine are much harder habits to kick than marijuana. According to Dale Archer, a clinical psychiatrist and author, it is up to the individual to use pot in a reasonable way. "It simply means that users will need to take charge of the amount and frequency of their use of this controversial drug, just like they should do with alcohol, saturated fats and sugar," Archer says. "That's not such a bad thing—it's called personal responsibility."[22]

Some heavy users do develop a psychological dependence on marijuana and subsequently find quitting difficult. But this is true of many substances that are legal to use, including alcohol and cigarettes. Psychological dependence generally occurs only with the small percentage of users who are actually abusing the drug, not with casual users. American culture certainly has contributed to the idea of marijuana addiction with terms such as *stoner* and *pothead*, which suggest a stereotypical user who does nothing but sit around in a bathrobe smoking pot and watching television all day. The truth is that pot smokers can become addicted to their behavior just as people grow addicted to food, sex, or gambling. They return to the drug to experience pleasure, to trigger the same reward centers in the brain, and if they have addictive personalities they may fall into harmful patterns of abuse. Longtime pot smokers generally take abstinence breaks to avoid dependence issues or problems with tolerance to the drug. At any rate, this type of dependence is scarcely comparable to the horrors of addiction to hard drugs.

> "Users will need to take charge of the amount and frequency of their use of this controversial drug, just like they should do with alcohol, saturated fats and sugar. That's not such a bad thing—it's called personal responsibility."[22]
>
> —Dale Archer, a clinical psychiatrist and author.

Concerns about addiction to higher-potency marijuana—as in some of the varieties made available through legalization—are also misguided. While it is true (according to the University of Mississippi's Research Institute of Pharmaceutical Sciences) that the strength of marijuana has increased slightly over the years, it is important to remember that more potent forms are not necessarily more hazardous or addictive. There is no risk of a fatal overdose from smoking pot, no matter its THC content. In fact, more potent weed may actually be safer, allowing users to get the desired high with fewer puffs, thus minimizing harm from taking in carcinogens from smoking.

Marijuana Is Less Addictive than Other Substances

Marijuana is much less addictive than other widely used substances. The graph shows the percentage of people who have tried a substance and then developed a dependency at some point. Marijuana has less addictive potential than legal substances such as tobacco and alcohol.

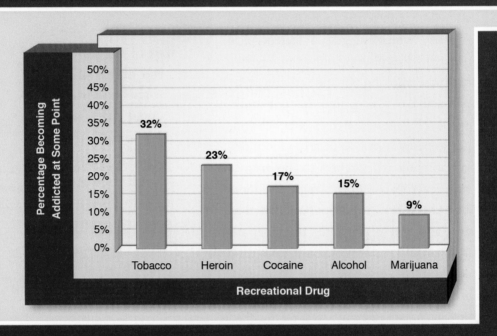

Addiction Potential of Recreational Drugs

Source: Leaf Science, "4 Myths About Marijuana Addiction," November 28, 2013. www.leafscience.com.

A Small Percentage of Addiction

According to the United Nations' 2012 World Drug Report, marijuana is the world's most widely used illicit substance, yet addiction rates for the drug remain small. Studies suggest that 9 percent of marijuana users become hooked. Yet it is instructive to compare this figure to the rate of addiction for other substances that are legal. About 15 percent of those who try alcohol become dependent, as do about 32 percent of those who try tobacco. Marijuana's rate is roughly equal to that for caffeine. Moreover, the 9 percent figure for marijuana is probably inflated. In surveys, users are considered to have a dependency problem if they spend considerable time and effort to obtain the drug. Yet this extra time and effort has been due almost entirely to pot being illegal and more difficult to get. Legalization would make it easy to purchase the drug—and it would also eliminate a category of supposedly addicted users.

It is easy to see why these exaggerated claims and statistics about marijuana addiction persist. As *High Times* magazine columnist Russ Belville puts it, "Marijuana addiction, just what is it? The simple answer is that marijuana addiction is a scary talking point for the prohibitionists clinging to their jobs against the growing wave of marijuana legalization."[23]

Not a Gateway Drug

Research has shown repeatedly that marijuana is not a gateway drug that causes users to try more dangerous substances. For frustrated supporters of legalization, this is the myth that will not die. The argument goes that people who begin smoking marijuana are lured into a false sense of security about drug use and progress to using harder drugs that are harmful. According to current statistics, 107 million Americans have tried marijuana—representing 40 percent of the population born since 1960—yet only 37 million have tried cocaine and only 4 million have taken heroin. Nearly every study has found that marijuana use does not cause subsequent usage of harder drugs. Instead, there is a correlation in some cases that

> "Marijuana addiction, just what is it? The simple answer is that marijuana addiction is a scary talking point for the prohibitionists clinging to their jobs against the growing wave of marijuana legalization."[23]
>
> —Russ Belville, a columnist for *High Times* magazine.

is only logical: those who have a craving to get high and are predisposed to try hard drugs probably begin with marijuana. But that does not mean that smoking weed somehow leads them to become heroin addicts.

Most hard drug users probably also smoked tobacco and drank alcohol at an early age, yet cigarettes and alcohol are not blamed for later drug use. And maybe alcohol should be blamed. A study published in the peer-reviewed *Journal of School Health* discovered that the gateway effect often associated with marijuana use is actually more prevalent with alcohol. This study of a national sampling of high school seniors found that students who use alcohol have a greater likelihood of moving on to both licit and illicit substances. According to the study's authors, "The findings from this investigation support that alcohol should receive primary attention in school-based substance abuse prevention programming, as the use of other substances could be impacted by delaying or preventing alcohol use."[24]

Both sides of the marijuana debate can agree that adolescent drug use is undesirable and should be discouraged. However, antilegalization voices often go further and spread fears that younger students who try marijuana are progressing quickly to other drugs. Yet a recent survey by NIDA found that while marijuana use among adolescents has increased in the past few years, use of heroin, cocaine, and methamphetamine has declined. Millions of Americans try pot when they are young and become casual users for years afterward with no ill effects. It is time to retire the idea of marijuana's gateway effect once and for all.

Legalization Could Reduce Addiction

Ironically, legalizing marijuana could actually lead to less addiction. Marijuana users shopping in legal outlets that sell pot exclusively would be less tempted to try other drugs, as they might be when purchasing marijuana from street dealers. In a paper debunking the gateway theory, the Marijuana Policy Project declares,

> In fact, some researchers believe that it is marijuana's illegal status that is the real gateway. Because marijuana is illegal, those who seek to buy it must obtain it from criminal drug dealers who often maintain an inventory of other drugs and have an incentive to expand their market to new users. This exposure to the illicit market—and peer groups that are willing to engage in drug use—can lead individuals to use of more dangerous drugs.[25]

This notion is supported by results from Portugal, which decriminalized all drugs in 2001. While technically still illegal, drug possession and usage in Portugal was reduced from a criminal offense to an administrative violation, like a parking ticket. Critics waited for the policy change to bring about a flood of new addicts, but this never happened. Drug usage rates for marijuana and other substances remained roughly the same and even decreased slightly in some areas. Money previously spent on enforcement of drug laws was placed instead into drug treatment efforts, which helped heavy users combat addiction. Like Portugal's successful program, legalizing marijuana in the United States could be a positive step toward a more rational drug policy overall.

Chapter Three

Does Using Marijuana Present Health Risks?

Marijuana Use Presents Significant Health Risks

- Heavy marijuana use can affect healthy brain development in teenagers.
- Marijuana use can increase the risk of heart attack and long-term cardiovascular disease.
- Using marijuana can cause anxiety, fear, or panic, particularly in those with a mental illness such as schizophrenia.
- Smoking marijuana can cause lung problems because of the carcinogens in pot and because pot smokers tend to inhale more deeply and hold the smoke longer than tobacco smokers.
- The THC in marijuana has harmful effects, including suppressing the immune system.

The Debate at a Glance

Marijuana Use Does Not Present Significant Health Risks

- Large-scale studies have found no increased risk for lung cancer or upper airway cancer in pot smokers.
- What health risks there are from smoking pot can be eliminated by taking the drug in other ways, such as eating pot-infused baked goods.
- Compared to alcohol, a legal product, marijuana is much less addictive, less toxic, and less prone to cause dangerous behavior.
- The great majority of marijuana users take it only occasionally and in small doses, which reduces health risks.
- Although using pot can worsen mental illnesses such as schizophrenia, marijuana does not cause mental illness.

Marijuana Use Presents Significant Health Risks

"I think that what we are seeing is a little bit of wishful thinking in the sense that we want to have a drug that will make us all feel good and believe that there are no harmful consequences. . . . If you are an adolescent and you are taking marijuana, there is a higher increased risk for addiction and there is also a higher risk for long-lasting decreases in cognitive capacity—that is, lowering of IQ."

—Nora Volkow, the head of the National Institute on Drug Abuse.

Quoted in Ruth Marcus, "The Myths of Smoking Pot," *Washington Post*, June 24, 2014. www.washington post.com.

Consider these questions as you read:

1. How persuasive is the contention that legalized marijuana presents a serious health hazard for young people? Explain.
2. Which health risk related to marijuana use do you think is most worrisome? Explain.
3. Should people with a history of mental illness be prevented from obtaining marijuana in states where it is sold legally? Why or why not?

Editor's note: The discussion that follows presents common arguments made in support of this perspective, reinforced by facts, quotes, and examples taken from various sources.

Media reports in the United States increasingly portray marijuana as a virtually harmless substance. Yet those who use marijuana actually face a variety of health risks, both short term and long term. Of particular concern to health care professionals are risks to young pot users. Many important developmental changes occur during adolescence. Young people in this period are expanding their intellectual abilities and developing vital social skills. "Adolescence is a sensitive time for brain development," says Matthew J. Smith, an assistant professor of psychiatry and behavioral sciences at Northwestern University's Feinberg School of Medicine. "If a teen introduces the abuse of marijuana at that point in their life, it could have consequences for their ability to problem solve, for their memory and for critical thinking in general."[26]

Smith's recent research is highlighting this danger. A study he and fellow researchers published in 2013 found that teens who smoked pot daily for about three years had unusual changes in their brain structures associated with working memory. Memory-related structures in the marijuana users' brains appeared to shrink and collapse inward, showing a likely decrease in neurons. The result was a pattern of poor performance on memory tests. Researchers noted that working memory is vital not only for academic success but also in everyday activities. Even more alarming was the study's finding that the brain structure abnormalities and memory problems persisted two years *after* the heavy users had stopped smoking weed. "The surprising finding is that we actually saw any shape differences," says Smith, "because one could hypothesize that after two years of abstinence the brain might start to heal itself. This evidence suggests that it may not necessarily do that."[27]

Despite such findings, marijuana use is widespread among secondary school students and not uncommon for younger students. A 2012 Monitoring the Future study discovered that 45 percent of twelfth-graders in the United States had tried marijuana, and 23 percent had used it within the last month. Sixty percent of high school seniors considered marijuana to be safe. A survey in Washington, conducted before that state legalized

> "Adolescence is a sensitive time for brain development. If a teen introduces the abuse of marijuana at that point in their life, it could have consequences for their ability to problem solve, for their memory and for critical thinking in general."[26]
>
> —Matthew J. Smith, an assistant professor of psychiatry and behavioral sciences.

Mood and Anxiety Disorders Associated with Marijuana Dependence

Dependence on marijuana often accompanies other mental and emotional health problems. People who abuse marijuana are much more likely to experience a variety of mood and anxiety disorders than the general population.

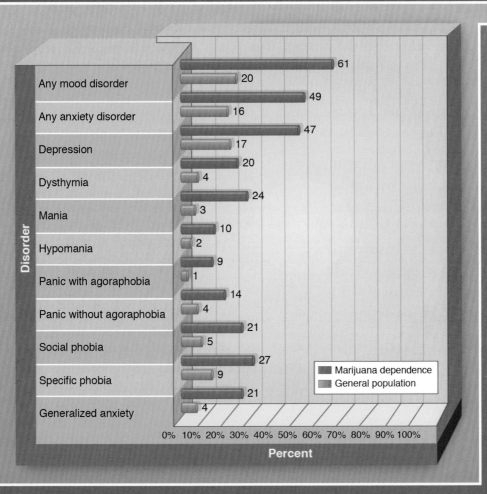

Mood and Anxiety Disorders Among Respondents with Marijuana Dependence

Disorder	Marijuana dependence	General population
Any mood disorder	61	20
Any anxiety disorder	49	16
Depression	47	17
Dysthymia	20	4
Mania	24	3
Hypomania	10	2
Panic with agoraphobia	9	1
Panic without agoraphobia	14	4
Social phobia	21	5
Specific phobia	27	9
Generalized anxiety	21	4

Percent

Source: NIDA, "Topics in Brief: Marijuana," December 2011. www.drugabuse.gov.

41

the drug for recreational use, found that a majority of tenth-graders there already found it easy to obtain pot. With legalization and relaxed attitudes, this ease of access will doubtless only increase—despite rules about minimum age for purchase. (Buyers must be at least twenty-one in Washington and Colorado.) New questions about marijuana's effect on adolescent brains demonstrate the folly of legalizing this dangerous substance.

A Risk of Heart Attack

Health risks from using marijuana are not limited to adolescents. The drug can produce short-term effects that are dangerous for any user. For example, a study by Boston's Beth Israel Deaconess Medical Center determined that the risk of heart attack within the first hour of smoking a joint is five times greater than that for nonsmokers. The risk increases with age and is compounded if the smoker is overweight or has heart or lung problems associated with smoking cigarettes. NIDA points out that marijuana can raise a user's heart rate by 20 to 100 percent shortly after the first puff, an effect that can persist up to three hours.

"There is now compelling evidence on the growing risk of marijuana-associated adverse cardiovascular effects, especially in young people."[28]

—Emilie Jouanjus, the lead author of a French study on possible links between marijuana use and symptoms of serious cardiovascular disease.

There are also long-term cardiovascular risks. In a recent French study, cardiologists warned about possible links between marijuana use and symptoms of serious cardiovascular disease, including heart attack, stroke, and circulation problems. Writing in the *Journal of the American Heart Association*, Emilie Jouanjus, the lead author of the French study, says cardiologists should consider whether heart problems in patients who use marijuana might be caused by the drug. "There is now compelling evidence on the growing risk of marijuana-associated adverse cardiovascular effects, especially in young people,"[28] says Jouanjus. Dr. Sherief Rezkalla, who cowrote an editorial on the subject for the American Heart Association journal, thinks researchers need to look more closely at safety issues with marijuana. According to Rezkalla, "It is the responsibility of the medical community to determine the safety of the drug before it is widely legalized for recreational use."[29]

Marijuana-Related Emotional and Psychological Problems

In addition to heart risks, marijuana use can have profound effects on a person's mental and emotional health. Research shows that pot can cause feelings of anxiety, fear, and panic, particularly in those with a mental illness such as schizophrenia. In fact, scientists are discovering a troubling relationship between schizophrenia and marijuana. Years ago it was thought that marijuana could trigger psychosis in most users. This idea was ridiculed by pot advocates, who caricatured it as the equivalent of the 1936 cautionary film *Reefer Madness*, in which wild-eyed teenagers smoked weed and behaved in a deranged fashion. Yet new research at the Institute of Psychiatry at King's College in London, England, has found genetic links between marijuana and certain forms of mental illness. "We know that cannabis increases the risk of schizophrenia," says Robert Power, who led the study. "Our study . . . suggests that there is likely to be an association in the other direction as well—that a predisposition to schizophrenia also increases your likelihood of cannabis use."[30] Power's work supports an earlier British study that found that pot smokers who begin at a young age have a dramatically increased risk of psychotic symptoms, and continued marijuana use increases the risk of developing a psychotic disorder later in life.

Robin Murray, a professor at the Institute of Psychiatry, views marijuana users who are prone to schizophrenia as a vulnerable minority. "Not only are there people suffering from psychosis who would not be in in-patient beds if they were not using cannabis," said Murray in 2004, "but use of the drug also drastically reduces the chances of recovery. People who do improve go out on the streets, meet their old dealer, begin using the drug again and relapse."[31] Murray's work led to marijuana being rescheduled as a more dangerous drug in Great Britain.

A recent study from the University of Pennsylvania also contradicts the notion of marijuana as a relaxing drug that promotes sleep. Researchers discovered that marijuana users actually have higher rates of sleep deprivation and restlessness. Those who began smoking pot before age fifteen were twice as likely to experience severe loss of sleep, even if they rarely used the drug later in life.

The Risks for Lung Damage

Long-term marijuana use may also be harmful to the lungs. Pot smokers tend to inhale the smoke more deeply, and the joints they smoke are unfiltered. Marijuana smoke also contains a number of carcinogens that can increase cancer risks for heavy users. The American Lung Association notes that there are thirty-three cancer-causing agents in marijuana; when equal amounts of tobacco and marijuana are smoked, the marijuana deposits four times as much tar into the lungs. A recent Canadian study tracking a large group of Swedish men over forty years suggests that heavy use of marijuana may as much as double the risk of contracting lung cancer. In a 2012 report entitled *The Impact of Cannabis on Your Lungs*, the British Lung Foundation noted that smoking pot posed a substantial hazard to the lungs and urged further investment in studies on how marijuana affects lung function. The authors of the report wrote, "We recommend that public health education programmes be implemented to dispel the myth that smoking cannabis is relatively safe, and to highlight the adverse respiratory effects of smoking cannabis mixed with tobacco."[32]

The Negative Effects of THC

Ironically, for a drug touted for use with HIV/AIDS patients, marijuana may actually inhibit the immune system, making users more susceptible to some infections and cancers. Findings published in the December 2010 *European Journal of Immunology* suggest that cannabinoids in the marijuana plant, including THC, trigger massive production of special immune cells that suppress immune response. Such a reaction may have some benefit with certain conditions, such as arthritis and MS, but it is counterproductive for cancer patients and those with diseases of the immune system. THC is also known to be damaging to prenatal brain cells. Children whose mothers smoked marijuana during pregnancy have a greater risk of stunted growth and may develop attention deficit/hyperactivity disorder, anxiety, and depression in later years.

Physicians' concerns about the health risks of marijuana—such as THC's effect on the immune system—seem to be contradicted by certain books and websites that promote pot as a panacea for all sorts of conditions, from breast cancer to HIV/AIDS. While more research is needed, people should approach such rosy claims with skepticism.

Marijuana Use Does Not Present Significant Health Risks

"Among adults [who screen positive for drug use] . . . we were unable to detect an association between frequency of marijuana use and health, emergency department use, or hospital utilization."

—Dr. Daniel Fuster is at Boston University's Department of Medicine.

Dr. Daniel Fuster et al., "No Detectable Association Between Frequency of Marijuana Use and Health or Healthcare Utilization Among Primary Care Patients Who Screen Positive for Drug Use," *Journal of General Internal Medicine*, September 19, 2013. http://link.springer.com.

Consider these questions as you read:

1. Which argument about the lack of health risks from using marijuana do you find most persuasive? Explain.
2. How important are arguments about pot being relatively less harmful than alcohol in the overall debate about legalization? Explain.
3. From the evidence presented, do you agree that the link between marijuana use and schizophrenia has been exaggerated? Why or why not?

Editor's note: The discussion that follows presents common arguments made in support of this perspective, reinforced by facts, quotes, and examples taken from various sources.

Smoking pot does not increase lung cancer risk—at least not with light to moderate use. That is the verdict of the foremost expert on the subject, Donald P. Tashkin, a professor with the David Geffen School of Medicine at the University of California, Los Angeles (UCLA). Tashkin has been studying marijuana and its impact on the lungs for more than thirty years. Several years ago Tashkin set out to prove that marijuana was harmful by conducting a meticulous study funded by NIDA. To his surprise, Tashkin discovered no link between moderate use of pot and risk of lung cancer, a finding that he published in a groundbreaking 2006 report. Tashkin recently affirmed these results in a review of similar studies from around the world. Writing in the *Journal of the American Thoracic Society*, Tashkin declares, "Findings from a limited number of well-designed epidemiological studies do not suggest an increased risk for the development of either lung or upper airway cancer from light or moderate use." He also emphasizes that smoking tobacco—a product that is legally obtainable everywhere—presents far more risks of lung problems than smoking pot. "In summary," he writes, "the accumulated weight of evidence implies far lower risks for pulmonary complications of even regular heavy use of marijuana compared to the grave pulmonary consequences of tobacco."[33] (*Pulmonary* is the medical term for lung-related issues and functions.) Tashkin also notes that THC in marijuana has tumor-reducing properties and may actually kill cancer-producing cells. This may account for the surprising lack of cancer in marijuana smokers despite the carcinogens in pot smoke.

> "Findings from a limited number of well-designed epidemiological studies do not suggest an increased risk for the development of either lung or upper airway cancer from light or moderate use."[33]
>
> —Donald P. Tashkin, a professor at UCLA's David Geffen School of Medicine.

Statistics and studies from the National Cancer Institute and the *Journal of the American Medical Association* generally support Tashkin's findings, although evidence about heavy pot smokers remains inconclusive. Advocates for legalizing marijuana (among whom Tashkin now numbers himself) complained in 2006 that the US government and the media either underplayed or completely ignored Tashkin's study. However, subsequent studies with similar results, along with Tashkin's influential review, have been widely discussed in the debate about legalization. For casual users the message seems clear: smoke in moderation, stay away from tobacco, and your chances of getting lung cancer are no greater than those of a nonsmoker.

Alcohol Seen as More Harmful than Marijuana

Large majorities of Americans view alcohol as much more harmful to individual health and to society in general than marijuana. Even if marijuana were as readily available as alcohol, which it is not, public attitudes toward marijuana and alcohol remain essentially unchanged.

	Which is more harmful to a person's health?			If marijuana were as widely available, which would be more harmful to society?		
	Alcohol %	Marijuana %	Both/ Neither %	Alcohol %	Marijuana %	Both/ Neither %
Men	67	17	13	63	24	10
Women	70	14	14	63	22	13
White	70	15	13	64	22	11
Black	80	9	9	79	14	6
Hispanic	57	21	21	47	32	18
18–29	81	12	6	76	18	5
30–49	71	17	11	67	22	10
50–64	67	14	15	61	25	12
65+	50	19	25	43	31	20
College grad+	66	18	12	63	23	10
Some college	75	13	10	67	21	10
HS or less	66	15	17	60	25	14
Republican	59	24	14	51	36	11
Democrat	76	11	10	74	16	9
Independent	70	13	15	62	22	13

Source: Pew Research Center, "Section 2: Views of Marijuana—Legalization, Decriminalization, Concerns," April 2, 2014. www.people-press.org.

Using Marijuana Without Smoking It

While fears about getting cancer from smoking marijuana are overblown, there are legitimate concerns about other harmful effects from smoking the drug. For example, it can irritate bronchial tubes and cause congestion and coughing. For those who experience these problems, there are many other ways to get the effect of marijuana without lighting up and puffing.

One of the most popular alternate methods is similar to smoking but healthier: using marijuana in vaporized form. A vaporizer works by heating the cannabinoids in pot to their boiling temperature. Rather than burning the buds and producing clouds of smoke, a vaporizer dehydrates the buds and causes them to release their effect without ever catching fire and exposing the smoker to carcinogens from the burning buds, paper, and air. The vaporizer method also eliminates many of the unpleasant by-products of smoking, such as ashes, resin buildup, and odor. In Colorado, where marijuana is now legal, entrepreneurs are already selling vaporizers to pot users. One company, Open Vape, makes a vaporizer that is similar to an e-cigarette, with a pen-like cylinder that heats a cartridge filled with purified cannabis oil.

Cannabis also can be ingested and is popular in candies, cookies, and butters. Edible marijuana was once notorious for varying wildly in potency. "People used to be afraid of edibles," says Bob Eschino, the head of a marijuana chocolate firm in Lakewood, Colorado. "You would eat an edible one day, you would have a great time. You would eat the same edible from the same person the next day, and it would be way too much medication. Nobody tested anything."[34] Today, however, laws in Colorado and Washington require strict testing and consistency. Some think these edible products will someday rival joints as the preferred way to enjoy the drug.

Vaporizers and edibles are just two of the smokeless methods for using cannabis. Other companies are marketing marijuana as rubs, tinctures, suppositories, and concentrates. So far, sales of these alternative forms are booming.

Less Harmful than Alcohol

When opponents of legalized marijuana insist that it is a dangerous substance, advocates counter by saying it is no more harmful than another widely used—and legal—product: alcohol. One person who agrees with the latter point of view is US president Barack Obama. In a 2014 *New*

Yorker interview, the president referred to his own pot-smoking days and said, "I don't think it is more dangerous than alcohol."[35] In fact, according to a recent Pew Research Center poll comparing attitudes about alcohol and marijuana, 69 percent of Americans believe alcohol is more dangerous to individual health, and 63 percent believe it is more dangerous to society in general. The National Institute on Alcohol Abuse and Alcoholism says that alcohol is the most commonly used addictive substance in the United States. No one is suggesting a return to Prohibition days, when alcohol was illegal. Yet the idea of legalizing marijuana for recreational use drives some critics into a frenzy.

Apart from alcohol's greater addictive qualities, it is more harmful than pot in other ways. Drunken drivers are responsible for huge numbers of fatalities and injuries on the nation's roads. Reduced inhibition from drinking leads to risky sexual behavior, which can involve catching sexually transmitted diseases and result in unplanned pregnancies. Alcohol is responsible for many long-term health problems, including liver disease. Alcohol abuse causes about eighty-eight thousand deaths per year—about half from chronic problems and the other half from acute incidents such as alcohol poisoning or fatal crashes. It is doubtful that even should marijuana become legal nationwide, it would result in so many problems and so many deaths.

Most Marijuana Use Is Occasional

Legalizing marijuana is unlikely to change the pattern of use for Americans. Most people who smoke pot smoke it only on occasion. According to a 2012 National Survey on Drug Use and Health, only about 17 percent of past-year users (those who had smoked pot in the last year) used marijuana on a daily or almost daily basis. *Rolling Stone* magazine reports that between 40 and 50 percent of people who have tried pot have used it fewer than twelve times in their entire lives. Casual users may light up a joint or consume a marijuana brownie once a week or even more infrequently. For many users, it is scarcely different from having an occasional cocktail. Opponents of legalization often act as though every pot smoker is or quickly will become an obsessive daily user. Surveys about patterns of use tell a very different story.

Marijuana Does Not Cause Schizophrenia

Recent studies that supposedly have found links between marijuana use and schizophrenia have been misrepresented to make the results sound more sensational. The key point of the research is that mental illness may lead to using pot, not the opposite. Most quoted is a King's College study of more than two thousand people, about half of whom reported having smoked marijuana. Researchers analyzed the participants' genetic profile, searching for known variations associated with schizophrenia. Those with the strongest genetic predisposition for schizophrenia were also more likely to use marijuana and to use greater amounts.

Robert Power, who headed the study at the Institute of Psychiatry at King's College in London, sees the results not as a wake-up call about pot but rather as an example of the interaction between a person's genes and his or her environment. Power pointed out that certain environmental risks, such as using marijuana, may be more likely given an individual's innate behavior and personality, which in turn are influenced by the person's genetic makeup. A related study from Harvard Medical School comparing families with a history of schizophrenia and those without also showed little support for the idea that marijuana causes schizophrenia. The researchers declared, "While cannabis may have an effect on the age of onset of schizophrenia it is unlikely to be the cause of illness."[36] Studies like these may finally put to rest fears about marijuana smoke leading to mental illness. As the public becomes better informed about current research, a more rational view of marijuana's limited health risks should prevail.

> "While cannabis may have an effect on the age of onset of schizophrenia it is unlikely to be the cause of illness."[36]
>
> —Researchers at Harvard Medical School comparing families with a history of schizophrenia and those with no such history.

Chapter Four

Does Legalizing Marijuana Benefit Society?

Legalizing Marijuana Benefits Society

- Legalizing marijuana would allow state and local governments to collect taxes from sales.
- Legalizing marijuana would free up tax dollars now squandered on law enforcement efforts against pot possession and use.
- Roads would become safer because marijuana impairs drivers less than alcohol.
- Legalizing marijuana would diminish drug violence and other crime.

The Debate at a Glance

Legalizing Marijuana Does Not Benefit Society

- Tax revenues from the sale of marijuana are overhyped and would be offset by higher social costs.
- Legalizing marijuana will lead to increased access and use for young people, who suffer more ill effects from the drug, including a drop in IQ.
- Legalizing marijuana will lower its price and lead to increased use.
- Car accidents will increase if people can legally buy and use marijuana.

Legalizing Marijuana Benefits Society

"We expect that the legalization of recreational marijuana in Colorado and Washington will lead to increased marijuana consumption coupled with decreased alcohol consumption. As a consequence, these states will experience a reduction in the social harms resulting from alcohol use. . . . On net, we predict the public-health benefits of legalization to be positive."

—Economists D. Mark Anderson of Montana State University and Daniel Rees of the University of Colorado.

Quoted in Jacob Sullum, "Economists Predict Marijuana Legalization Will Produce 'Public-Health Benefits,'" *Forbes*, November 1, 2013. www.forbes.com.

Consider these questions as you read:

1. How persuasive is the case that legalized marijuana will produce a huge amount of new tax revenues? What could upend these expectations? Explain.
2. Do you agree that money spent previously on pursuing those who broke marijuana laws was squandered? Why or why not?
3. Do you think that if marijuana were legalized nationwide, drug gangs and cartels would be put out of business? Explain.

Editor's note: The discussion that follows presents common arguments made in support of this perspective, reinforced by facts, quotes, and examples taken from various sources.

One huge benefit of legalizing marijuana is a flood of new tax dollars. This outcome is already apparent in Colorado, the first state in which stores are legally able to sell marijuana products for recreational use. Buyers twenty-one and older can buy and possess no more than an ounce at one time, yet revenues have been brisk. Each buyer pays 12.9 percent in state sales taxes and a 15 percent excise tax. Altogether these taxes added almost $11 million to state coffers by the end of April 2014, just four months after legal sales began. The Drug Policy Alliance, a Denver-based group that advocates drug reform, expects Colorado's tax revenues for the first year under the new law to be about $40 million.

While the $40 million figure is undoubtedly impressive, state officials actually expect that number to grow rapidly as the industry expands. Money from marijuana taxes is already earmarked for school construction and social programs in Colorado. Marijuana is also proving to be good for the Colorado economy in other ways. With pot sales expected to approach $1 billion for the 2014 fiscal year, the state has added ten thousand jobs in the industry. The number of retail shops has expanded from the 24 that opened on January 1, 2014, to more than 150 statewide by early July. New businesses are cropping up, such as a software firm that markets a seed-to-sale tracking system for marijuana growers. Tourism is stronger than ever. All this good news has impressed Colorado voters as well. Although the new law was approved by a margin of only 10 percent in 2012, polls say voters now favor it by a margin of 22 percent. Not even the relatively high tax rates can dampen supporters' enthusiasm. "Sure, the taxes are a little bit too high. But we've been asking for this for 40 years," says Robert Kane, vice president of a Colorado Springs company that makes cannabinoid medical products. "I'll gladly pay an extra $5 or $10 every time I go to the store to shop in a regulated market and have the money go to my kids' schools. Let's do this, get the establishment started, show the world we can do this in a responsible way."[37]

Politicians in other states are doubtlessly looking on with keen interest and imagining all the great things they could do with a large new

> "I'll gladly pay an extra $5 or $10 every time I go to the store to shop in a regulated market and have the money go to my kids' schools. Let's do this, get the establishment started, show the world we can do this in a responsible way."[37]
>
> —Robert Kane, the vice president of a Colorado Springs company that makes cannabinoid medical products.

source of tax revenue. Marijuana proponents have also been pleased at other aspects of Colorado's experiment. "There was this hushed anticipation of what might happen . . . but the sky didn't fall," says Amanda Reiman, the California policy manager for the Drug Policy Alliance, which is working to legalize recreational pot in the Golden State. "We didn't see people quitting their jobs and becoming lazy stoners. We didn't see kids dropping out of schools by the hundreds. We didn't see people peddling pot in schoolyards."[38] Experts say that taxing legal marijuana nationwide at rates comparable to those on alcohol and tobacco could raise about $8.7 billion in revenue for federal, state, and local governments. It probably will not be long before other states vote to legalize marijuana and benefit from the potential windfall of tax revenues.

Money Saved on Law Enforcement

Another tax advantage of legalizing marijuana is the ability to spend tax dollars on more vital areas of law enforcement than chasing down pot smokers. As the authors of *Marijuana Is Safer: So Why Are We Driving People to Drink?* put it, "Law enforcement resource allocation is a zero-sum game. Every hour—or to be more accurate, hours—police officers spend arresting and processing minor marijuana offenders is time they are not out on the streets protecting the public from more significant criminal activity."[39] Most people agree that the endless so-called war on drugs has been an expensive failure in the United States. Despite decades of antimarijuana public service messages and massive police efforts, casual marijuana use continues unabated.

Legalization can save a huge amount of government money now being squandered on enforcing outdated laws on pot. Savings would be realized throughout the criminal justice system, from police to courts to corrections facilities. Since about 750,000 people are arrested annually in the United States for possession of pot, the impact of changing marijuana laws would be immediate and sweeping. In a 2010 analysis, Jeffrey Miron, a senior economics lecturer at Harvard University, estimated that legalizing marijuana nationwide would save almost $9 billion a year in law-enforcement expenditures. Award-winning journalists Alyson Martin and Nushin Rashidian think that policy changes are long overdue:

> The end of cannabis prohibition will mark the beginning of the end of the war on drugs—which has been, at its core, a war on cannabis and cannabis users. . . . Once the human and financial costs of cannabis prohibition are removed from the picture—halting unnecessary arrests, preserving law enforcement hours and efforts, and saving billions—a rational and more manageable conversation about the remains of the drug war can emerge.[40]

Safer Roads

Opponents of legal marijuana also feed irrational fears about driving safety. They conjure images of stoned potheads causing mayhem on streets and highways. In reality, however, drivers under the influence of marijuana are much less of a problem than drunk drivers. A recent study from Denmark, published in the online journal *Accident Analysis & Prevention*, confirms that pot is consistently safer than most other substances that cause impaired driving. The study found that the highest risk for accidents with severe injury was associated with alcohol use, alone or with other substances. The drug that was least risky for serious accidents was cannabis.

This is not to say that driving while impaired by marijuana is perfectly safe or desirable. State and local laws regarding driving under the influence of marijuana will probably have to be reviewed in the coming age of legalized cannabis. However, a great deal of research suggests that smoking or ingesting marijuana causes less psychomotor-skill impairment than alcohol, amphetamines, and many other drugs. Researchers say the difference in risk between pot and alcohol is mainly due to the fact that drunken drivers tend to drive faster than normal and overestimate their driving skills, but stoned drivers tend to do the opposite. Also, whereas marijuana smokers tend to use the drug at home, drinkers are often out at bars and have to get home by car. If legalized marijuana leads to more use of pot and less drinking, US roads will undoubtedly become safer.

State governments can benefit from a flood of new tax dollars
due to legalized marijuana. The marijuana industry is projected
to generate as much as $8 billion in sales by 2018. This amount
would be subject to state taxes and fees, providing a steady
stream of new revenue for states with legalized pot.

US Marijuana Sales Estimates 2013–2018 in Billions of US Dollars

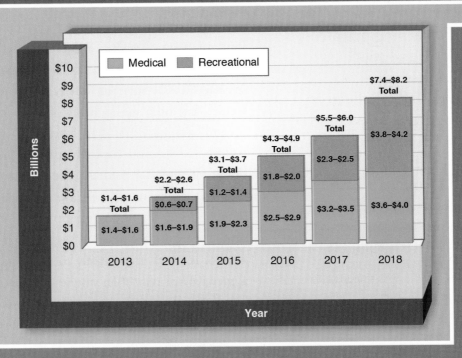

Source: MMJ Business Daily, "New Forecast: U.S. MMJ and Recreational Cannabis Sales to Hit $8 Billion by 2018,"
April 9, 2014. http://mmjbusinessdaily.com.

A Reduction in Drug-Related Violence and Other Crime

Legalizing marijuana could also make American cities and towns safer
by reducing drug violence and drug-related crimes. In states where pot
is illegal, gangs and cartels can make considerable profits selling marijuana. In protecting their turf, these criminal syndicates often engage in

violence that can spill over and harm innocent victims. According to the Marijuana Policy Project website,

> The only reason such criminal gangs make any money at all from marijuana is that our current policies allow them to. By keeping marijuana illegal and confined to the black market, our wildly ineffective marijuana laws—and any elected official who supports them—are to blame for handing criminals a virtual monopoly on the lucrative marijuana trade.[41]

> "By keeping marijuana illegal and confined to the black market, our wildly ineffective marijuana laws—and any elected official who supports them—are to blame for handing criminals a virtual monopoly on the lucrative marijuana trade."[41]
>
> —The Marijuana Policy Project, an organization that advocates legalizing marijuana.

Legalizing pot may also reduce other kinds of violence, such as domestic abuse. Researchers at the University of Tennessee and Florida State University recently found that odds of aggressive behavior toward romantic partners increased in college-age men on days when the men drank alcohol. By contrast, the authors reported, "marijuana use days did not increase the odds of any type of aggression."[42] Decades of research suggest that alcohol is much more likely to result in aggressive behavior than smoking cannabis. If people turn to legal marijuana in place of alcohol, it stands to reason that violent episodes will be reduced.

Early statistics from Colorado indicate that legalization is already having a positive effect on crime in that state. Policy makers in other states should look at the benefits of reducing crime and violence that come from legalizing marijuana.

Legalizing Marijuana Does Not Benefit Society

"Marijuana companies, like their predecessors in the tobacco industry, are determined to keep lining their pockets. Indeed, legalization has come down to one thing: money. And it's not money for the government—Colorado has only raised a third of the amount of tax revenue they have projected—it's money for this new industry and its shareholders."

—Kevin A. Sabet, a former White House drug policy adviser and the director of Smart Approaches to Marijuana.

Kevin A. Sabet, "Colorado's Troubles with Pot," CNN, July 10, 2014. www.cnn.com.

Consider these questions as you read:

1. Some insist that the extra tax revenues produced by legalized marijuana will be offset by the social costs of abuse and addiction. Do you agree? Explain.
2. Large tobacco companies drew increasing criticism when their product proved to be dangerous to the public health. Do you believe the same thing could happen with marijuana growers and sellers? Why or why not?
3. Do you agree with the assertion that legalized marijuana will result in more underage users? Explain.

Editor's note: The discussion that follows presents common arguments made in support of this perspective, reinforced by facts, quotes, and examples taken from various sources.

Supporters of legalizing marijuana make great claims about the enormous tax revenues that will come rolling in with the new laws. So far the actual revenues from pot sales in Colorado have been far less than the pie-in-the-sky predictions tossed around when the law was being debated. State officials have already scaled back projections of tax revenue in the first year from $150 million to $40 million. Some cannabis users continue to buy on the untaxed black market. Others are trying to remain in the medical marijuana system, which taxes marijuana at a lower rate and thus reduces revenue. Many cities and counties, including Colorado Springs, are refusing to license retail pot stores. And the uncomfortable truth is that much of whatever revenue is collected will be offset by costs of various kinds. One cost the public seems to overlook is the expense of running a vast new system for selling and regulating marijuana—a system the likes of which never has been set up in the United States. "I don't think [legal marijuana] is the savior for state budgets," says Phyllis Resnick, the lead economist at the Denver-based Colorado Futures Center of Colorado State University. "It brings in additional revenue, but it also brings in additional costs for administration of the system and regulation and monitoring. It's not free money."[43]

Colorado governor John Hickenlooper anticipates that enforcement costs will offset a good deal of tax and fee revenue from legalization. Hickenlooper insists, however, that the state's main responsibility is to address problems such as more pot-impaired drivers, underage users, and individuals who become dependent. Solutions require more tax dollars. Experience shows that the tax revenues generated from alcohol and tobacco sales are far outweighed by the social costs of addiction and abuse. Daniel Okrent, who is an expert on prohibition in America, says, "[People] indulging a fantasy of income tax relief emerging from a cloud of legalized marijuana smoke should realize that it is likely only a pipe dream."[44] Marijuana legalization also brings with it other social costs, including withdrawal, mental illness, and missed work. These are harder to quantify, but they add to the true price tag of legalized pot.

> "[People] indulging a fantasy of income tax relief emerging from a cloud of legalized marijuana smoke should realize that it is likely only a pipe dream."[44]
>
> —Daniel Okrent, an author and expert on prohibition in America.

Yet another effect that will offset revenues is the end to property forfeitures from drug dealers. In Washington, which also has legalized marijuana, the state's drug task force must now deal with funding shortfalls. The drug-fighting group has historically depended on funding from cash, houses, cars, and other assets seized from lawbreaking pot dealers. The task force has already slashed its budget for 2014 and must now make do with less money for overtime, training, and new equipment. Washington voters earmarked marijuana tax revenues for everything from education to substance abuse prevention, but they gave none to law enforcement. Experts say property seizures from other types of drug cases will not fill the void. "The advantage with marijuana is that it's one location, and you can make a lot of money off of one grow," says Matthew York, a Seattle attorney who handles forfeiture cases. "These other drug dealers, they make a lot of money, but they're harder to find."[45]

More Underage Users

Legalizing marijuana will result in more underage users. Whereas society once sought to keep kids away from drugs and dealers, now it is sending the message that drug use is fine. Statistics show that past-month use of pot by twelve- to seventeen-year-olds has been highest in states that have legal medical marijuana. This problem will only grow worse with legalization for recreational use. When parents and guardians can legally keep pot in the household, it provides a danger-ous example for youth and tempts them to experiment with the drug. Christian Thurstone, a youth-addiction researcher at the University of Colorado, Denver, observes that his clinic has been "inundated with young people reporting for marijuana-addiction treatment. . . . Every day, we see the acute effects of the policy of legalization. And our kids are paying a great price."[46]

Edible pot packaged as candy bars, lollipops, and other treats is par-ticularly dangerous to kids. In the first five months of legalization in Colorado, nine children required care at the state's largest pediatric emer-gency department for accidentally eating marijuana products. Seven of the children had to be admitted to the hospital's intensive care unit, and one child needed a respirator. Some lawmakers are appalled that busi-nesses are manufacturing edible pot products that resemble candy and

The Denver City Council expects costs related to legalizing marijuana (including for enforcement, regulations, health, and education) to be greater than projected revenues from taxes and fees. Supporters of legalization tend to downplay or ignore these substantial costs.

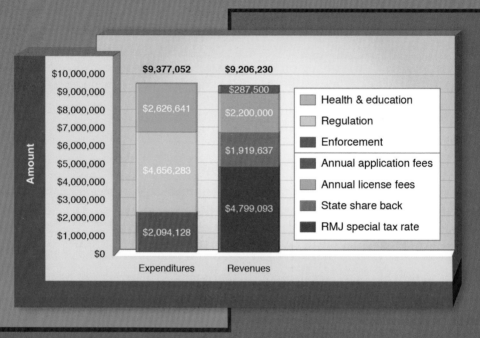

Source: *Westword*, "Marijuana: Denver's Projected Revenues from Recreational Pot Won't Cover Expenditures," July 9, 2013. http://blogs.westword.com.

have an obvious appeal for children. "Marijuana edibles are dangerous in the hands of kids," said Colorado state representative Frank McNulty, who cosponsored a tougher new law about packaging edibles. "That has become all too familiar to the people who work here at Children's Hospital."[47] Experts warn that marijuana has a damaging effect on very young users—whether it is smoked or ingested. Use of the drug can interfere with healthy brain development, and over time it may actually lower an individual's IQ. Pot advocates simply urge adults to keep their stash away from children. Yet with the lax standards of legalization, this is much easier said than done. No doubt the new marijuana retailers hope to recruit young users to expand their trade in the future. The sad truth is that they are more concerned with profits than the safety of children.

Falling Prices, Increased Use

In another nod to economics, marijuana retailers in Colorado and Washington have worried about keeping their prices competitive with black-market sellers. In both states the price early on was high, due to large demand and a small supply. However, as demand levels off and supply from private growers expands, prices will certainly fall—and perhaps too much, says UCLA public policy professor Mark Kleiman. As Washington's policy consultant on legalized marijuana, Kleiman is very influential, and he believes pot prices could soon become dangerously low, which in turn could lead to heavier use, especially among price-conscious young people. Once the market stabilizes, the cost of producing a gram of marijuana could go as low as fifty cents. Even with taxes and regulatory fees added on, the price could be well below the street value

> "Marijuana edibles are dangerous in the hands of kids. That has become all too familiar to the people who work here at Children's Hospital."[47]
>
> —Colorado state representative Frank McNulty, the cosponsor of a bill about packaging edible pot more responsibly.

of illegal pot. "The main bad outcome from cannabis legalization, the only one that I think matters, is an increase in heavy use, and particularly heavy use among minors," Kleiman says. "The strongest policy lever to prevent additional drug abuse is to keep prices up."[48] Kleiman sees further problems coming from potential marijuana advertising, which would only reinforce young people's relaxed attitudes toward pot and other drugs. Spreading the idea of marijuana as a cheap and legal high would have bad consequences for society as a whole.

The Dangers of Driving High

Legalizing marijuana will also make the nation's roads and highways less safe. Marijuana proponents insist that drivers high on pot are more capable than drunken drivers. But a driver under the influence of marijuana is still an impaired driver, with less ability to react and to rapidly attend to multiple factors as required in safe driving. The fact is that pot is responsible for many accidents and personal injuries. In 2011, for example, marijuana was involved in 455,668 emergency room visits across the nation, according to a report from the Drug Abuse Warning Network.

A recent study from Columbia University's Mailman School of Public Health found that fatal automobile crashes involving marijuana have tripled in the United States. "Currently, one of nine drivers involved in fatal crashes would test positive for marijuana,"[49] says Dr. Guohua Li, the director of the Center for Injury Epidemiology and Prevention at Columbia and the coauthor of the study. Li also found that the risk of a fatal crash was twenty-four times greater than that for a sober person if the driver is under the influence of both alcohol and marijuana. As yet, police do not have a fast and accurate test for marijuana intoxication as they do for alcohol. Should pot-related crashes increase due to legalization, public demand for such a test and for other law-enforcement measures will certainly increase. Jan Withers, the national president of Mothers Against Drunk Driving (MADD), sees driving while high as a worrisome trend. "MADD is concerned anytime we hear about an increase in impaired driving, since it's 100 percent preventable," says Withers. "When it comes to drugged driving versus drunk driving, the substances may be different but the consequences are the same—needless deaths and injuries."[50]

Source Notes

Overview: Legalizing Marijuana

1. Quoted in Michael Martinez, "Colorado's Recreational Marijuana Stores Make History," CNN, January 1, 2014. www.cnn.com.
2. Quoted in Jack Healey, "After 5 Months of Sales, Colorado Sees the Downside of a Legal High." *New York Times*, May 31, 2014. www .nytimes.com.
3. *Wellness Letter*, "The Times They Are A-Changin'," June 2014. http:// BerkeleyWellness.com.
4. Quoted in Stephen Siff, "The Illegalization of Marijuana: A Brief History," *Origins: Current Events in Historical Perspective*, May 2014. http://origins.osu.edu.

Chapter One: Should Marijuana Be Prescribed for Medical Use?

5. Jerome P. Kassirer, "Editorial: Federal Foolishness and Marijuana," *New England Journal of Medicine*, January 30, 1997. www.marijuana library.org.
6. John Fauber, "Pot a Common Remedy to Ease Back Pain," Medpage Today, October 11, 2013. www.medpagetoday.com.
7. Sanjay Gupta, "Why I Changed My Mind on Weed," CNN Health, August 8, 2013. www.cnn.com.
8. Quoted in Evan Williams, "For the Reefer," *Naples Florida Weekly*, December 12, 2013. http://naples.floridaweekly.com.
9. Quoted in Kelly Johnston, "A Cancer Patient's Journey with Medical Marijuana," *Metro Times*, September 25, 2013. http://metrotimes .com.
10. Quoted in Deborah Kotz, "Marijuana Can Alleviate MS Symptoms," *Boston Globe*, April 28, 2014. www.bostonglobe.com.
11. National Institute on Drug Abuse, "DrugFacts: Marijuana," January 2014. www.drugabuse.gov.

12. Quoted in Cassie Shortsleeve, "The Truth About Medical Marijuana," *Men's Health*, April 24, 2013. www.menshealth.com.

13. Quoted in Melissa Healy, "Potential for Heart Attack, Stroke Risk Seen with Marijuana Use," *Los Angeles Times*, April 23, 2014. http://touch.latimes.com.

14. Quoted in David E. Newton, *Marijuana: A Reference Handbook*. Santa Barbara, CA: ABC-CLIO, 2013, p. 149.

15. Henry D. Jampel, "Should You Be Smoking Marijuana to Treat Your Glaucoma?," Glaucoma Research Foundation, June 25, 2013. www.glaucoma.org.

Chapter Two: Will Legalizing Marijuana Lead to Increased Addiction?

16. Quoted in Foundation for a Drug-Free World, "The Truth About Marijuana." www.drugfreeworld.org.

17. Quoted in Maia Szalavitz, "Is Marijuana Addictive? It Depends How You Define Addiction," *Time*, October 19, 2010. http://healthland.time.com.

18. Kristin Mastre, "The Art of the Tolerance Break," *Budding Fort Collins* (blog), April 19, 2013. http://buddingfortcollins.com.

19. National Institute on Drug Abuse, "DrugFacts."

20. Quoted in Rachael Rettner, "Marijuana Withdrawal Is Real, Study Says," Live Science, September 26, 2012. www.livescience.com.

21. Quoted in Ron Snyder, "Experts Debate Whether Marijuana Is a 'Gateway' Drug," ABC2 News, February 16, 2014. www.abc2news.com.

22. Dale Archer, "Is Marijuana Addictive?," *Psychology Today*, May 5, 2012. www.psychologytoday.com.

23. Russ Belville, "What Is Marijuana Addiction?," *High Times*, June 6, 2014. www.hightimes.com.

24. Quoted in Arjun Walia, "Study: The 'Gateway Drug' Is Alcohol, Not Marijuana," Collective Evolution, April 12, 2014. www.collective-evolution.com.

25. Marijuana Policy Project, "Is Marijuana a 'Gateway Drug'?" www.mpp.org.

Chapter Three: Does Using Marijuana Present Health Risks?

26. Quoted in Randye Hoder, "Why It's Still a Big Deal If Your Teen Smokes Pot," CNN Health, January 28, 2014. www.cnn.com.

27. Quoted in *Northwestern Magazine*, "Memory Goes Up in Smoke," Spring 2014. www.northwestern.edu.

28. Quoted in Healy, "Potential for Heart Attack, Stroke Risk Seen with Marijuana Use."

29. Quoted in Healy, "Potential for Heart Attack, Stroke Risk Seen with Marijuana Use."

30. Quoted in Kate Kelland, "Study Finds Genetic Links Between Schizophrenia and Cannabis Use," Reuters, June 24, 2014. www.reuters.com.

31. Quoted in Steve Boggan, "If Cannabis Is Safe, Why Am I Psychotic?," *Times*, January 7, 2004. www.timesonline.co.uk.

32. British Lung Foundation, "The Impact of Cannabis on Your Lungs," 2012. www.blf.org.uk.

33. Quoted in Tim Sandle, "Smoking Marijuana Might Not Cause Lung Cancer . . . and Could Even Fight It," *Medical Marijuana Review*, July 3, 2013. http://medireview.com.

34. Quoted in Celia Watson Seupel, "6 Ways to Get High Without Actually Smoking," *Huffington Post*, February 28, 2014. www.huffingtonpost.com.

35. Quoted in David Remnick, "Going the Distance: On and Off the Road with Barack Obama," *New Yorker*, January 27, 2014. www.newyorker.com.

36. Quoted in John M. Grohol, "Harvard: Marijuana Doesn't Cause Schizophrenia," PsychCentral, December 10, 2013. http://psychcentral.com.

Chapter Four: Does Legalizing Marijuana Benefit Society?

37. Quoted in Kristen Wyatt, "Marijuana's Tax Potential Attracts New Allies," *Denver Post*, November 6, 2013. www.denverpost.com.

38. Quoted in Josh Richman, "Marijuana Legalization in Colorado: So Far, So Good," *San Jose Mercury News*, July 6, 2014. www.mercury news.com.

39. Steve Fox, Paul Armentano, and Mason Tvert, *Marijuana Is Safer: So Why Are We Driving People to Drink?* White River Junction, VT: Chelsea Green, 2013.

40. Alyson Martin and Nushin Rashidian, *A New Leaf: The End of Cannabis Prohibition*. New York: New Press, 2014, pp. 218–19.

41. Marijuana Policy Project, "It's Not the Marijuana but Its Prohibition That Fuels Crime," 2014. www.mpp.org.

42. Quoted in Paul Armentano, "Alcohol Fuels Domestic Violence, While Marijuana Doesn't—Guess Which One the Feds Are Demonizing," AlterNet, January 9, 2014. www.alternet.org.

43. Quoted in Jennifer Oldham, "Colorado Pot Revenue Lags Forecasts as Licensing Is Slow," *Bloomberg Businessweek*, May 1, 2014. www .businessweek.com.

44. Quoted in Smart Approaches to Marijuana, "Tax Revenue Use." http://learnaboutsam.org.

45. Quoted in Zusha Elinson, "Pot Legalization Crimps Funding of Drug Task Forces," *Wall Street Journal*, January 9, 2014. http://on line.wsj.com.

46. Quoted in Sheila Polk, "Legalized Marijuana: Colorado Kids Are Paying the Price," AZ Central, January 6, 2014. www.azcentral.com.

47. Quoted in John Ingold, "Children's Hospital Sees Surge in Kids Accidentally Eating Marijuana," *Denver Post*, May 21, 2014. www.den verpost.com.

48. Quoted in Gabriel Spitzer, "Washington's 'Pot Czar' Says Legal Marijuana Could Be Too Cheap," KPLU 88.5, March 10, 2014. www .kplu.org.

49. Quoted in CBS Seattle, "Study: Fatal Car Crashes Involving Marijuana Have Tripled," February 4, 2014. http://seattle.cbslocal.com.

50. Quoted in CBS Seattle, "Study."

Marijuana Facts

Marijuana Use and Laws

- According to the 2012 National Survey on Drug Use and Health, marijuana is the most commonly used illicit drug in the United States. The survey showed that 18.9 million Americans aged twelve or older had used marijuana in the month before the survey. That figure represents 7.3 percent of the total population.
- A 2013 survey by the Pew Research Center shows that nearly half of all adult Americans (48 percent) have tried marijuana.
- More than 63 percent of Americans would be bothered to see people smoking marijuana in public, according to a 2014 Pew Research Center survey. On the other hand, about 57 percent said they would not be opposed to a store or business selling marijuana in their neighborhood.
- Besides Colorado and Washington, which have legalized marijuana for recreational use, fifteen other states have decriminalized possession of small amounts of pot.
- According to the National Organization for the Reform of Marijuana Laws, about 740,000 people in the United States are arrested each year on marijuana charges. Few people charged with simple possession end up in jail. Most who are jailed for marijuana offenses are guilty of selling the drug.

Medical Marijuana

- As of mid-2014, twenty-three states and the District of Columbia had passed laws legalizing marijuana for medical use. The first state to pass such a law was California in 1996. Maryland, Minnesota, and New York passed medical marijuana laws in 2014.
- In states where medical marijuana is legal, the approved treatments for its use vary widely. The amount that people can possess also varies. According to ProCon.org, in Alaska, the limit is 1 ounce (28 g), but in Washington State it is 24 ounces (680 g).

- There are more than twenty-three hundred medical marijuana dispensaries in the United States, reports the legal website Nolo.com.
- The FDA does not classify marijuana as a pharmaceutical. Officially, the federal government still considers marijuana to be an illegal narcotic. However, the FDA and the federal government allow state programs to proceed.
- In 2005 the US Supreme Court ruled in *Gonzales v. Raich* that any person who grows, possesses, or distributes medical marijuana, regardless of state laws, is in violation of federal antimarijuana laws and is subject to federal prosecution.

Negative Factors

- Politifact.com, a Florida-based website, estimates that less than 5 percent of people using medical marijuana in programs around the country actually have cancer, glaucoma, or HIV. Most treatments are for vague claims of pain or discomfort.
- According to NIDA, one in six young people who use marijuana will develop a dependency and may suffer structural brain damage as a result of heavy use.
- Testing sponsored by the federal government and conducted at the University of Mississippi's Potency Monitoring Project, indicates that the average potency of marijuana (as measured by levels of THC) has risen steadily for three decades and now exceeds 10 percent.
- Public health officials interviewed by the *Huffington Post* warn that the ability to harvest marijuana crops legally could lead to many unregulated and inexperienced growers using dangerous pesticides on their crops. These unwelcome chemicals can add to the dangers of smoking or ingesting cannabis.

Positive Factors

- Legalization will end the disparity in marijuana possession arrests that have disproportionately affected minorities. For example, according to the American Civil Liberties Union, African Americans are almost four times more likely to be arrested for marijuana than whites, even though they use the substance at similar rates.

- A 2012 study by the Mexican Institute of Competitiveness contends that legalization of marijuana in Colorado could reduce Mexican drug cartels' earnings from illegal sales by as much as 30 percent. Violence related to these groups could also diminish.
- Americans for Safe Access, an advocacy group for therapeutic marijuana, says that legalization will make it easier for scientists to perform research on marijuana as a medication. This could lead to new insights about its positive effects and potential uses.
- Robin Room, the director of Australia's Centre for Alcohol Policy Research, says that the ability to purchase and use marijuana legally may reduce binge drinking in young people. Binge drinking (five or more drinks in two hours for men; four or more for women) is associated with alcohol poisoning, serious injuries, automobile crashes, and other problems.

Related Organizations and Websites

American Medical Marijuana Society

phone: (914) 210-3988

e-mail: medicalmarijuanasociety@yahoo.com

website: http://medicalmarijuanasociety.org

The American Medical Marijuana Society supports growers, suppliers, distributors, and patients of medical marijuana in its mission to see the medicinal use of marijuana legalized nationally.

Americans for Safe Access

1806 Vernon St. NW

Washington, DC 20009

phone: (202) 857-4272

e-mail: info@safeaccessnow.org

website: www.safeaccessnow.org

Americans for Safe Access works to ensure safe and legal access to marijuana for therapeutic uses and research.

Cato Institute

1000 Massachusetts Ave. NW

Washington, DC 20001

phone: (202) 842-0200

website: www.cato.org

The Cato Institute is a public-policy research organization—a think tank—devoted to the principles of individual liberty, limited government, free markets, and peace. Its scholars and analysts conduct independent, nonpartisan research on a wide range of policy issues.

Citizens Against Legalizing Marijuana (CALM)
PO Box 2995
Carmichael, CA 95608
phone: (916) 965-4825
e-mail: carladlowe@aol.com
website: www.calmca.org

Citizens Against Legalizing Marijuana is an all-volunteer political action committee dedicated to defeating any effort to legalize marijuana in California and throughout the United States. CALM believes that federal laws against the use, cultivation, and transportation of marijuana should be maintained and enforced.

Drug Enforcement Administration (DEA)
8701 Morrissette Dr.
Springfield, VA 22152
phone: (202) 307-1000
website: www.justice.gov

The mission of the Drug Enforcement Administration is to enforce the controlled substance laws and regulations of the United States. The DEA also recommends and supports nonenforcement programs aimed at reducing the availability of illicit controlled substances on the domestic and international markets.

Drug Free America Foundation, Inc.
5999 Central Ave., Suite 301
St. Petersburg, FL 33710
phone: (727) 828-0211 • fax: (727) 828-0212
e-mail: webmaster@dfaf.org
website: http://dfaf.org

The Drug Free America Foundation, Inc., is a drug prevention and policy organization committed to developing, promoting, and sustaining national and international policies and laws that will reduce illegal drug use and drug addiction.

Marijuana Policy Project (MPP)
PO Box 77492
Washington, DC 20013
phone: (202) 462-5747
e-mail: info@mpp.org
website: www.mpp.org

The Marijuana Policy Project works to increase public support for nonpunitive, noncoercive marijuana policies and to change state laws to reduce or eliminate penalties for the medical and recreational use of marijuana.

National Cannabis Industry Association
1718 M St. NW, #377
Washington, DC 20036
phone: (888) 683-5650
e-mail: communications@thecannabisindustry.org
website: https://thecannabisindustry.org

The National Cannabis Industry Association seeks to promote the growth of a responsible and legitimate cannabis industry. It also works for a favorable social, economic, and legal environment for that industry in the United States.

National Institute on Drug Abuse (NIDA)
6001 Executive Blvd., Room 5213, MSC 9561
Bethesda, MD 20892
phone: (301) 443-1124
e-mail: webmaster@nida.nih.gov
website: www.drugabuse.gov

The mission of the National Institute on Drug Abuse is to lead the nation in bringing the power of science to bear on drug abuse and addiction. NIDA supports and conducts research across a broad range of disciplines and uses the results to improve prevention and treatment of drug abuse and addiction.

National Organization for the Reform of Marijuana Laws (NORML)
1100 H St. NW, Suite 830
Washington, DC 20005
phone: (202) 483-5500 • fax: (202) 483-0057
website: http://norml.org

The mission of the National Organization for the Reform of Marijuana Laws is to influence public opinion sufficiently to legalize the responsible use of marijuana by adults. NORML also serves as an advocate for consumers so that they have access to high quality marijuana that is safe, convenient, and affordable.

For Further Research

Books

Jonathan P. Caulkins et al., *Marijuana Legalization: What Everyone Needs to Know.* New York: Oxford University Press, 2012.

Steve Fox, Paul Armentano, and Mason Tvert, *Marijuana Is Safer: So Why Are We Driving People to Drink?* White River Junction, VT: Chelsea Green, 2013.

Alyson Martin and Nushin Rashidian, *A New Leaf: The End of Cannabis Prohibition.* New York: New Press, 2014.

David E. Newton, *Marijuana: A Reference Handbook.* Santa Barbara, CA: ABC-CLIO, 2013.

Roger Roffman, *Marijuana Nation: One Man's Chronicle of America Getting High.* New York: Pegasus, 2014.

Kevin A. Sabet, *Reefer Sanity: Seven Great Myths About Marijuana.* New York: Beaufort, 2013.

Periodicals

Niraj Chokshi, "There's More than One Way to Legalize Marijuana," *Washington Post,* July 8, 2014.

Dan Frosch, "Colorado Grapples with Risks from Edible Marijuana," *Wall Street Journal,* May 9, 2014.

Randye Hoder, "Why It's Still a Big Deal If Your Teen Smokes Pot," *Time,* January 23, 2014.

Olga Khazan, "Why Marijuana Should Be Legal, and Expensive," *Atlantic,* July/August 2014.

Rick Lyman, "Pivotal Point Is Seen as More States Consider Legalizing Marijuana," *New York Times*, February 26, 2014.

Jacob Sullum, "How Is Marijuana Legalization Going? The Price of Pot Peace Looks Like a Bargain," *Forbes*, July 10, 2014.

Internet Sources

Drug Policy Alliance, "Marijuana Legalization and Regulation," 2014. www.drugpolicy.org.

The Scientist, "Is Cannabis Really That Bad?," January 23, 2013, www.the-scientist.com.

WebMD, "Marijuana Use and Its Effects," 2012. www.webmd.com.

Index

Note: Boldface page numbers indicate illustrations.

Accident Analysis & Prevention, 56
addiction
    to marijuana vs. narcotic painkillers, 15
    physical vs. psychological, 27
    potential of marijuana vs. other drugs,
        34
alcohol
    impairs drivers more than marijuana
        does, 56
    marijuana is less harmful than, 49–50
    marijuana legalization may reduce binge
        drinking of, 71
    views on harm from, vs. marijuana use,
        48
Allsop, David, 29–30
American Academy of Neurology, 18
American Civil Liberties Union, 70
Americans for Safe Access, 71
Anderson, D. Mark, 53
anorexia nervosa, 17
Anslinger, Harry J., 10
anxiety/anxiety disorders
    associated with marijuana dependence,
        41
    marijuana can cause, 22, 28, 43
    marijuana can relieve, 8, 20
appetite, marijuana stimulates, 8, 17
Archer, Dale, 32–33
arrests, annual, for marijuana charges, 69
Azzariti, Sean, 6

Belville, Russ, 35
Boyd, J. Wesley, 32
brain
    addiction/dependence and, 27, 33
    desensitization of cannabinoid receptors
        in, 28
    marijuana abuse can impede
        development of, 40, 62

prenatal, THC is damaging to, 44
British Lung Foundation, 44

cannabidiol (CBD), 8
chemotherapy, 16–17
Christie, Chris, 19
Collen, Mark, 15
Controlled Substances Act (1970), 10, 20
crime, drug-related, marijuana legalization
    would reduce, 57–58

delta-9-tetrahydrocannabinol (THC), 14
    may have tumor-reducing properties, 47
    negative effects of, 44–45
    physiological effects of, 8
    problems with controlling dose of,
        19–20
dependence, mood/anxiety disorders
    associated with, **41**
Distefano, Michael, 31
driving safety
    marijuana as lower risk to, 50, 56
    marijuana as risk to, 63–64
Drug Policy Alliance, 54
drug testing, 8

ElSohly, Mahmoud, 20
endocannabinoids, 14
Eschino, Bob, 49
European Journal of Immunology, 44

Fauber, John, 14
Florida State University, 58
Food and Drug Administration, US
    (FDA), 20, 70
Foundation for a Drug-Free World, 27, 28
Fuster, Daniel, 46

Gimbel, Mike, 31
Glaucoma Research Foundation (GRF),
    23
Gonzales v. Raich (2005), 70

Harm Reduction Journal, 15
Harvard Medical School, 51
hashish, 7, 8
health risks, 21–22
    of alcohol are greater than marijuana,
        49–50
    cardiovascular, 42–43
    debate over, 46
    to lungs, 21, 44
    marijuana use does not pose significant,
        46–49
Hickenlooper, John, 60

immune system, 22, 44
The Impact of Cannabis on Your Lungs
    (British Lung Foundation), 44

Jampel, Henry D., 23–24
Johnston, Anne, 17
Jouanjus, Emilie, 42
Journal of School Health, 36
Journal of the American Heart Association,
    42
Journal of the American Medical Association,
    47

Kane, Robert, 54
Kassirer, Jerome P., 14
Kleiman, Mark, 63
Kloner, Robert A., 22

law enforcement, marijuana legalization
    saves money on, 55–56
legalization
    as benefit to society, debate over, 52
    creates more underage users, 61–63
    creates revenue for states, 53–55
    reduced drug-related violence/crime,
        57–58
    revenues from, are overstated, 59–61
    saves money on law enforcement, 55–56
    will lead to more impaired drivers,
        63–64
Li, Guohua, 64
lung cancer/lung disease, 21, 44
    marijuana does not cause, 46–47

marijuana
    alcohol is less harmful than, 49–50

debate over health risks of, 38
does not cause schizophrenia, 51
edible, as risk to children, 61–63
emotional/psychological problems
    related to, 43–44
as gateway drug, **30,** 30–31
increase in potency of, 8, 20, 70
methods of consuming, 10
mood/anxiety disorders associated with
    dependence on, **41**
origin of term, 7
physical effects of, 8
prevalence of use in US, 69
states legalizing, **9**
used by most smokers only occasionally,
    50
withdrawal symptoms, 29–30
See also legalization; medical marijuana
marijuana burnout, 28
Marijuana Is Safer (Fox et al.), 55
marijuana laws, history of, 10–11
Marijuana Policy Project, 36, 58
Marinol, 17
Martin, Alyson, 56
Mastre, Kristin, 28
McNulty, Frank, 62, 63
medical marijuana
    benefits of, 14
    boosts appetite, 17
    debate over, 12
    disorders treated by, **21**
    is effective against nausea/vomiting,
        16–17
    is overhyped as medicine, 23–24
    is safer than narcotic painkillers, 15–16
    is step toward full legalization, 24
    potential sales of, **57**
    problems with smoking as delivery
        system, 20, 21
    relieves muscle tremors/spasms, 18
    support for use of, 14, **16**
memory, impact of marijuana on, 8, 22, 40
Miron, Jeffrey, 55
Monitoring the Future survey, 40
mood disorders associated with marijuana
    dependence, **41**
Mothers Against Drunk Driving (MADD),
    64
multiple sclerosis (MS), 18, 44

muscle tremors/spasms, marijuana relieves, 18

National Cancer Institute, 47
National Institute on Drug Abuse (NIDA), 19–20, 42, 70
  on marijuana withdrawal symptoms, 29
National Library of Medicine, US, 27
National Multiple Sclerosis Society, 18
National Organization for the Reform of Marijuana Laws, 69
National Survey on Drug Use and Health, 50, 69
New England Journal of Medicine, 14
Nolo.com (website), 70

Obama, Barack, 49–50
Okrent, Daniel, 60
opinion polls. *See* surveys
Oz, Mehmet, 13

pain relief
  marijuana is effective for, 13–14, 17
  marijuana is safer than narcotics for, 14–16
  percentage of marijuana users seeking, **21**
  traditional painkillers are more effective than marijuana for, 23
Parkinson's disease, 18
Pew Research Center, 69
Politifact.com (website), 70
Pollara, Ben, 14–15
polls. *See* surveys
Portugal, marijuana decriminalized in, 37
Power, Robert, 51
ProCon.org (website), 69
Proposition 215 (CA), 11

Rashidian, Nushin, 56
Reagan administration, 10

Reefer Madness (film), 10, 43
Rees, Daniel, 53
Reiman, Amanda, 55
Resnick, Phyllis, 60
Rezkalla, Sherief, 22, 42–43
Rolling Stone (magazine), 50
Room, Robin, 71

Sabet, Kevin A., 7, 23, 59
Schedule I drugs, 20–21
schizophrenia
  marijuana does not cause, 51
  marijuana increases risk of, 43
sleep, marijuana and problems with, 43–44
Smith, Matthew J., 40
surveys
  on harm from alcohol vs. marijuana use, **48,** 50
  of high school seniors on marijuana use, 40–41
  on marijuana for medical use, 14, **16**

Tashkin, Donald P., 46–47
tetrahydrocannabinol (THC). *See* delta-9-tetrahydrocannabinol
Thurstone, Christian, 61
tolerance breaks, 28

University of Tennessee, 58

Vandrey, Ryan, 26
vaporizers, 49
Volkow, Nora, 27, 39

war on drugs, 10, 55, 56
Weiner, Howard, 18
Withers, Jan, 64
World Drug Report, 34

York, Matthew, 61

362.295
ALL

Allen, John.

Thinking critically.
Legalizing
marijuana.

$28.95

DATE			

4-16   Ø

12/16   Ø

5/17   1

11/20   1   —

2/22   1   —

6/24   1   2/17

BAKER & TAYLOR